NEVER OFF DUTY

Never Off Duty is published under Voyage, a sectionalized division under Di Angelo Publications, Inc.

VOYAGE

Voyage is an imprint of Di Angelo Publications.
Copyright 2021.
All rights reserved.
Printed in The United States of America.

Di Angelo Publications
4265 San Felipe #1100
Houston, TX 77027

Library of Congress
Never Off Duty
ISBN:978-1-955690-00-3

Words: Nate Silvester
Cover Design: Savina Deianova
Interior Design: Kimberly James
Managing Editor: Cody Wootton
Editors: Ashley Crantas, Elizabeth Zinn, Stephanie Yoxen

Downloadable via Kindle, Nook, and Google Play.

For educational, business, and bulk orders, contact sales@diangelopublications.com.

1.Political Science --- Law Enforcement
2. Political Science --- Political Freedom
3.Biography & Autobiography --- Law Enforcement
4. Biography & Autobiography --- Personal Memoirs

NEVER OFF DUTY

NATE SILVESTER

CONTENTS

FOREWORD

I do not normally endorse books. However, this one is different. Simply put, I left this book feeling empowered. I felt spoken for. I felt like I had a voice. With his unique style of humor and real talk, Nate helps us all take steps toward achieving broader understanding. After reading Nate's words, you will better understand what officers go through day in and day out.

Police work is one of America's most misunderstood professions, period. There is no question in my mind regarding that.

One concept you'll realize after reading this book is that the life of a police officer is filled with a myriad of feelings, such as heroism, excitement, adrenaline, fear, uncertainty, and disappointment. Police officers experience a spectrum of emotions that would cause many people to go completely crazy, or to run as far from the job as they can get. Unfortunately, police in America have been under attack, which has exacerbated the negative aspects of police work.

What Nate has done with this book, and throughout his career as a police officer, could not have been more perfectly timed to give life to the dying spirit of police officers and those who love them. We must have a voice! Society must understand! This is not just a need, but a matter of life and death.

As the Progressive Left pushes to cancel us and more police chiefs are cowering by the minute, we need to take a stand. Once you finish reading this book you will understand why we need change. But then, what do you do about it? Do you get mad and cry, or do you act? Do you quit, or do you rise up and fight for what you own? Be active. Protest peacefully when necessary, vote for those who support cops, and contact city officials when you see injustice against officers. It's never a bad time to show love to your local officers. Do ride-alongs, tell an officer "Thank you," and, for those who have the passion to serve, become a police officer and be the change we need.

Enjoy the read, but make sure that, when you're finished hearing the truth, you stand.

- Officer Tatum

CHAPTER ONE
DON'T BE A COP

Don't be a cop.

Let me just get that right out there in the open before I discuss anything else, okay? I'm not just running my mouth here. In its current state, law enforcement is one of the worst possible career options you could consider. You might as well craft a literal bullseye target out of cardboard and glue it to your forehead. It's a minefield of endless blame, ridicule, and thanklessness. If you're on the fence about being a cop, get off the fence. Get far away from the fence and don't go near it anymore, because this job will not tolerate anything less than your utmost commitment and, if you're not on board with that, go play basketball and leave police work to the professionals.

Don't come lightly to this job. Come with full intent, or don't come at all.

You might know me as "nateswildn" from TikTok, but I'm Nathan Silvester from Twin Falls, Idaho. Most people just call me Nate. I was most recently employed with the Bellevue Marshal's Office in Bellevue, Idaho. I wasn't a perfect cop, because those don't exist; that's a lie we've been fed. But I was a good one. I served in law enforcement for about twelve and a half years, starting in 2006 with the Twin Falls Police Department. They sent me to the academy, where I graduated that same year and then worked with them until 2018, when I was fired due to a very strained relationship with the administration in the police department and with the city manager's office. Chances are, if you know a cop, you know someone who went down the same shit-chute that I did. You might not hear about them for any number of reasons, and I can't tell you their story. Not yet anyway.

All I can do is tell you mine. All I can do is show you the perspective I've gained and trust that someone, somewhere, will hear me out.

My first encounter with a police officer was when I was about fifteen years old and newly licensed. I was just leaving the Twin Falls County Fair and pulled out onto a residential street, going kind of fast because I had a lead foot. One of the local cops stopped me, but he didn't end up giving me a citation. What I remember most clearly is him saying, "I don't want to catch you driving like a bat out of hell again."

For whatever reason, that one-liner stuck very vividly in my mind. I had broken the law, but this guy was more like a miffed uncle or older brother. Why was he so casual? Aren't cops supposed to be super professional? Shouldn't I be in cuffs by now? I'd gotten a stern warning, which got the point across, but no citation to take home and have to explain to my dad. He hadn't nailed me to the floor on my first offense. He spoke my language and it worked. I thought it was humane of him to just give me a warning, and I left that exchange feeling grateful.

Toward a cop.

I'd grown up influenced by those who thought that police officers were calloused, jaded hard-asses just looking for an excuse to haul me and my loved ones off to jail. If you were unlucky enough to get a cop's attention, you got busted on the spot. Even if you were innocent, they'd find or fabricate some law you'd broken so they could fill their quotas and laugh about it all the way to the donut shop. That's how the "real" cops were. Thugs with guns. Five-O. The Fuzz. Po-po. Pigs.

God, I hate these names.

How had I miraculously gotten a decent cop when the overwhelming majority of them were supposedly bad apples?

As my number of interactions with police officers increased over the years (lead foot hard at work), I started to realize that some of these cops *might actually be people.* Somewhere behind those aviators was a mind, maybe even a flash of humor; somewhere behind that badge was a heart. How strange to imagine, even for a moment, that these walking uniforms had emotions, or worries, or shortcomings like all the rest of us. Their days changed, shifts changed, temperaments changed, characteristics changed. This ebb and flow wasn't supposed to happen, at least not with the police. There wasn't room for humanity when the world was full of criminals.

But why the fuck would anyone want to be a cop, especially in this day and age?

I ask myself that question all the time, and it's complicated. When I was just a kid I always wanted to be a police officer. I saw the cops in the movies. *Bad Boys, Lethal Weapon, Beverly Hills Cop, Tango & Cash.* Fucking *Die Hard*—I can't tell you how many times I watched *Die Hard* growing up, but it might be 362 times, give or take. And, of course, they're Hollywood movies, so they made it look like a very glamorous job, right? You get to drive fast and shoot guns and take the bad guys off to jail. You high-five your partner and drive your Pontiac Firebird out of the station to the cheers of the adoring public. Then you go home to your beautiful girlfriend in your amazing apartment that's furnished with all this high-end quality stuff and bang her like a rock star. And I thought, *Wow, yeah, that would be really cool. I want to be a cop.*

My mom desperately tried to talk me out of it—because what parent wants their kid getting shot at—and it eventually worked. Over time, I slowly dismissed the notion of being an officer and went on to pursue other things. Jump ahead a number of years to when I was newly married and trying to make ends meet at an agricultural dealership. If you're curious, places like that sell combines, harrows, and windrowers; if none of that rings a bell, you probably don't need this information in your life, just like I didn't. That was one of the worst jobs I've ever had. It was just miserable, and it made me miserable to work there. It wasn't some meaningful, fulfilling job at all, but it was something that I could do, and I never paused to consider that I could do better for myself. It kept food on the table. It bought diapers. It paid the bills so I could occasionally afford to go out to dinner with my then-wife.

One such time, we came across a woman who used to babysit my wife, and she turned out to be an officer with the Twin Falls Police Department. She told us about her job and how she was enjoying it. And she looked at me and said, "You know, we're hiring. You should come fill out an application." I said, "Okay, my job right now is shit, so why not? I'll throw my hat in the ring for that." And I did. I filled out the application and they gave me the time and the date of the physical test, which took place before any other hiring procedures. It's a physically demanding job, so it makes sense that the physical test would come first, right? I wasn't in top condition, but I liked working out and had thrown discus and shot put in high school (still hold the discus record at Twin Falls, if you want to know). I thought I might have a chance.

I remember showing up and seeing about forty other applicants, and some of these guys were wearing their military workout gear. They had the words "Army", "Navy", or "Marine Corps" in huge letters on dark shirts. I looked around and thought, *What the hell am I doing here? These guys are way more qualified.* But I stuck around and completed the physical test. I passed, but I still expected to get shooed away any second. They announced that only four of us would be chosen, so, naturally, I started looking around and comparing myself all over again. How could I have a chance against all these military types? I wanted to bow out, but something said to stick around. My name got called for the interview and in I went. I was nervous as hell, but I answered each question as honestly as I could. I made it a point to be straightforward, flaws and all. Maybe they were just blowing smoke up my ass, but the panel said I gave one of the best interviews they had ever heard. But it was nice to hear that, and, one test after another, I just kept getting passed along the hiring process. Eventually, they offered me the job. I couldn't believe it. A career I could get behind. No more scrimping for baby food. No more ag store. No more farmers yakking about tractor parts and how much moisture we got back in '84.

Time to be a cop.

At that point, I didn't necessarily have a real passion for police work. I thought, *Well, this is going to be an experience. This is something different, something unknown.* To me, that was kind of exciting, but I also thought, *Why not? Why not police in the community I live in? Everybody wants to live in a safe community, so why don't I do my part to make mine safe? And what better way to do that than by actually putting on the badge and doing the work?* I had become the thing I so aspired to be as a boy, almost by accident, it seemed. I'd be sliding across car hoods with Riggs and Murtaugh in no time. This was the start of a new adventure, and being able to contribute to a safer community for me and my family was just icing on the cake.

If only it were so simple. For all the stars in my eyes, I couldn't fathom the toll of the journey I'd just begun, or the destructive impact it would have on me in the long run. I couldn't see the pain I'd have to endure for choosing to back the blue.

Years down the road, after being a cop for a while and getting canned for the first time, I took a three-year hiatus from law enforcement and tried to find that "next thing." I was already in good shape, so I did some personal training, some nutrition counseling, and some health consulting, but nothing felt quite right. Then, in the summer of 2020, a former coworker of mine at the Twin Falls Police Department, who happened to be the marshal in Bellevue, offered me a job. I initially turned it down because I had sort of put law enforcement in my rearview mirror. I'd already told myself, "That chapter of my life is over," and moved on. I'd spent twelve years in it and had learned a lot of things. I had experienced, like any job, the good and the bad, but there were so many memories I wished I could leave behind, too. And I felt, at that time, that law enforcement had already taken so much from me and hadn't given me much back in return, which, frankly, I don't think anybody really expects it to. The position came with a certain expectation of masochism, at least in my eyes, and at least as far as the mistreatment of officers by administrators. Whether it's one department or another, the top-down interference eventually spoils the pot.

My stint with TFPD was a period of my life that I was grateful for but didn't necessarily want to re-experience. I turned the job offer down, knowing that, if I took it, I'd have to put up with the same kind of excessive scrutiny and criticism I'd already endured—specifically, the micromanaging of egotistical administrators. So, I said "No," but she came back to me a couple of months later and said, "Hey, we're really hurting for people. I've worked with you. I know you're a good cop, and we need good cops in Bellevue right now." I don't want to say it was out of the kindness of my heart, but part of me did miss law enforcement, missed the work itself. And I knew in Bellevue, as has been so recently confirmed, that I'd have to deal with the bureaucracy and politics that tend to affect law enforcement, even in Podunk, Wherever. A little hesitant and a little hopeful, I took the job and started with the Bellevue Marshal's Office on December 1st of 2020, and that's where I was when I made a one-minute video on TikTok that changed my life forever. That's when the powers that be handed me a one-week suspension for calling out a blatant act of hypocrisy.

Who in their right mind would want to be a cop and put their livelihood, possibly even the lives of their family members, on the line? Who would willingly strap a target to their back for a thankless, high-pressure job where you're always the scapegoat? And what kind of people patrol our streets? The answer is: not quite who you think.

Try as we might, we're a society that thrives on stereotypes. If you disagree, that's fine, but it makes me wonder how much you're looking around. We think we know our neighbors, the other drivers on the road, even those we might consider our enemies. We assume things about schoolteachers, the people at the gas station, the cashier at the grocery store. We tell ourselves we've got them all figured out. Earned or not, these assumptions direct much of our daily interactions, from who we smile at to who we lash out at, and most of us don't have the wherewithal to stop for a moment and consider who's feeding everyone this misinformation, or why.

I'm not saying we're bad people—only that bad people are among us. They spread lies, overreact, and think volume equals winning. These things affect us as a country, and one of the worst outcomes is the impact on public perception of law enforcement. Right now, cops are the enemy—according to media, at least. Do a search for anything related to police and I'm willing to bet money you'll find a negative connection at the top of the results: almost entirely news reports with half the facts and all of the loud opinions. The real facts, the whole story, get tucked out of sight while mobs form and riots clash. Public and online forums alike collapse into chaos, spurred by knee-jerk reactions and wild accusations. Meanwhile, the cops—enemies of these zealots—are just trying to keep a lid on the whole thing so it doesn't boil over and kill everyone. These cops (the good ones, anyway), with their dwindling support from all sectors, are backed into their corners and told to keep quiet. So there they stay, silently calling for backup that isn't coming. They're calling and calling for help that won't arrive.

See, Mom had some foresight for little Nate back then. Nothing prophetic or mystic, just good common sense. She knew the dangers of the field and didn't want her son to be put in harm's way, and for good reason. What's your life worth to you? Because, at least in Idaho, the median salary for police work is forty-four grand a year. How many cops around the US die in the line of duty every month, or are put out of commission with permanent injuries? If you listen to some voices, the answer is, "Not enough!" Cops have always had a hard job, but there's no denying that things have taken a huge downward turn in 2021. The amount of media scrutiny and the popularity of demonizing police officers have risen to overwhelming proportions. Those silent calls for backup are fading into a sea of anger that grows with every lie. Quite simply, something's got to give.

And that's why I'm writing this now. That's why I'm standing up to raise my voice in defense of the more than 800,000 men and women who find themselves silenced behind the badge—for them, and their frightened families, and the unseen battles they fight to serve and protect. I can't do it on my own, which is why my hope is that this book will reach enough people willing to set aside their prejudices, their susceptibilities, and their overreactions to back the blue. So, I'm sorry, Ma, but I found my purpose, and I'm not backing down until we get that change we're looking for, the kind of change that keeps people safe no matter what side they're on. We're really hurting for people, and we need good people in the world right now.

CHAPTER TWO
DARK BLUE

I keep things from my loved ones.

It's not a matter of hiding the truth so much as holding it back. If you're in a first responder field, you know what I'm talking about. Shit happens, and it gets dark and it gets heavy. We see things that no one else has to endure, and then we have to find a place inside to compartmentalize everything and filter out all the bad during normal, everyday life. Except we end up keeping all that pain and confusion and anger and holding it inside to shield others from it, and it eventually takes its toll.

Officers are complex creatures, but I'd like people to see them for the good, decent humans they really are. The part that is difficult to explain is the switch that gets installed when you take that oath. The switch that gets flipped when things get raw and a cop has to stop being the nice guy for a while. Occasionally, the darkness inside must rise to the surface to respond to the darkness in the world. There is no other way to defeat the evil that exists other than to meet it with just as much, or more, severity. You have to be stronger than the opposition, and sometimes that means asking for more than anyone should give. Sometimes it takes everything you have and leaves nothing behind. Once the threat is gone, you close the darkness back up inside and become a "normal" person again.

Or at least that's what you hope happens.

My daughter is someone you'd be lucky to know. She's a light in my world. She's got a good heart and a good head, but I can't shake the feeling that maybe, just maybe, she'll come to me one day and say, "Dad, I want to be a cop like you." And as much as I'd like to tell her, "Hell no, you're going to college to get an education and do bigger, better, and safer things," she's her own person and can choose for herself...after she's heard some of the things I've kept from her about what I do. Right now, all she knows is that Dad goes and does police work. She doesn't see the things I've filtered out and shielded her from.

So, if she did want to look into being a cop, we'd have to sit down and have a long conversation about what the work involves physically, emotionally, and psychologically. I'd have to give her those details I've been holding back—at least enough to get the point across. I'd try to encourage her to do almost anything else, because her concept of what I do is sheltered. It's the edited-for-TV version, and it isn't grounded in reality.

Honestly, no one knows what cops' lives are like.

I got asked to speak to some students a while back, because Mom's a teacher and is retiring after thirty years, which is just awe-inspiring. Working thankless jobs must run in the family. Anyway, the kids asked me, "Is being a cop worth it? What should we do if we want to be police officers?" That put me in a tough spot, because the truth doesn't align with the public's perception, so I tried to walk that fine line of encouraging them to pursue their interests while avoiding any misleading language that could give an altruistic portrayal. I had to bullshit them, in other words. A lot of people get into this job thinking that it's exactly what they want, but they don't quite understand the day-to-day. It's not always exciting. We're not always rushing from crime scene to crime scene. There's a lot of downtime with police work, and sometimes it can be uneventful and monotonous—especially the paperwork. It's hard to feel like a rock star when you're entering traffic reports behind a computer screen for half a shift.

But then there's the other side of police work where you get called to a house and open the door to something you can't forget no matter how hard you try. Where the dad OD'd with his head in the toilet and the mom is convulsing on the living room couch while she tries to peel the skin off her forearms. Where you hear muffled crying in a back room and find a huddle of starving, filthy children sitting in feces with bruised ribs and empty eyes. And you have to pick up those kids—who still wail for their mother but cling to you *so tightly*—and carry them out one at a time to the waiting arms of strangers, where they'll get passed down the line and end up in foster care. And the saddest part of that is, the kids don't want to leave because it's all they've known. It's familiar for them, and going into something that's unfamiliar is somehow scarier than the nightmare they've just left. It breaks your heart because you know it's better than this living hell. How could it not be? But their hearts are breaking and they're scared because all they've seen of the world is the shitty, miserable life that was forced on them by their drug-addicted parents.

How do you deal with stuff like that? No, really, I'm asking you. Stop and think about this for a second.

Are you prepared to see a dead body and realize that was a human life that's over and done now? Whatever desires, aspirations, or goals they might have had are finished, bookended, and irreversible. And if that dead body is a child—or an infant—how is that going to affect you when the nights get quiet? What's your plan for keeping your shit together at a potluck six months later when you see a little girl get her arm yanked by an angry parent?

I'm going to share a story from my time as a detective, but I'm warning you now that it's grim and it's upsetting. It's not the made-for-TV version. I'm not sharing it for shock value, or to be dramatic; I'm sharing it because I promised myself I would show people what police work is really like. If you want to skip these next two paragraphs, I'm the last person who will blame you for that. I understand. Really, I do.

I was on call one particular night in December of 2014. I got called out to investigate a trailer fire. By the time I arrived at the trailer park, the fire department had already put the blaze out, but not in time to prevent two small boys—five years old and seven years old—from being consumed by the flames. They just weren't fast enough. The boys' bodies were transported to the emergency room and laid out on gurneys. I arrived there with my supervisor and an evidence technician. When I entered the room and pulled back the curtain to reveal the charred, still, lifeless bodies of those boys, I couldn't process what I saw. They were completely black, incinerated. The portions of their skin that weren't charred were red and disfigured. There wasn't a square inch of them that hadn't been burned. Most of their clothing had been scorched off by the fire, but I could still make out portions of action figures on what remained of their shirts. Then there was the dead, burned skin flaking off of their tiny hands and feet. I stifled my tears and the lump in my throat as I looked over at our evidence tech. She was taking photos of the boys with tears streaming down her face. Observing the autopsy, seeing the medical examiner slice into their bodies to make his way to the organs and determine the cause and manner of death, was worse. It's not a subtle or gentle process, this opening of tissue and bone to reach the truth. There are no "handle with care" instructions. These people are dead, and dead bodies during an autopsy are manhandled like a side of beef. I thought I was prepared for this because I'd attended other autopsies...of adults. This hit me in a different place, because I could only imagine that a day or so earlier these boys were alive, playing with their little sister and preparing for Christmas, which was only a few days away.

Now, my job as a detective was to determine whether or not this was an accident or a homicide. I had to interview their mother, and that may have been the hardest part of this investigation. I listened as she described the horror of the event. She lived in the camper trailer with her daughter and two boys. She'd gone outside to talk on the phone and the oldest of the boys locked the deadbolt on her as a prank. There was a space heater in the trailer and someone had left a blanket sitting too close to it. It caught fire, and it didn't take long for the small trailer to become fully engulfed. Mom tried to open the door to get her kids out, but the deadbolt was latched and the boys had retreated to the opposite end of the trailer to avoid the flames. Mom was able to pull her daughter, the smallest child, out through a tiny window, but the boys were trapped, huddled together, as the fire spread across the trailer toward them. They had nowhere to go. I listened as Mom described trying to break windows, clawing and punching at the trailer walls to get to her boys, who were crying out for her in pain as the fire overtook them. I looked down at Mom's hands, which were broken and bleeding. She could barely speak over her sobs. She had suffered burns of her own from being so desperately close to the burning trailer. This was no homicide, just an unimaginably horrific tragedy and loss.

At the time, my daughter was only a couple of years older than these boys. I went home and held her extra close that night. I managed to hide my emotions from her for the most part, until I was alone in my room. My daughter wasn't completely oblivious; she knew something bad had happened and wanted to know about it. Without giving her any of the details, I explained to her that two young boys had died and I had been called to investigate it. The location of the fire happened to be on my route to, and from, my house, and each time we passed it my daughter would ask a new question about the fire and the boys that had died. She felt that darkness and wanted to understand. Of course, I didn't share everything with her. I would now that she's older, to illustrate the reality of police work.

Maybe there are those of you reading this book who are new to law enforcement or plan on applying for an agency somewhere. Are you prepared for this level of heartache? Can you compartmentalize this kind of secondary trauma? Most importantly, if you can compartmentalize it, can you bring it to the surface again later and deal with it so it doesn't do any lasting damage way down deep in your psyche? And can you, after recognizing the damage, reach out to others for support?

There's a stigma about asking for help that needs to be dismantled. Officers will talk to each other about their traumatic work but, most of the time, the discussion just ends up becoming this commiserating humor; it never gets to the root of what's making them feel the way that they do. They joke about things like murder, domestic violence, drug addicts, and all the administrators who cheat on their spouses (I said what I said). Many officers turn to alcohol, and they turn to drugs. The suicide rate among police officers is way too high—not that there's an acceptable number—and it's getting higher and higher every year. They call it "gallows humor" for a reason.

If I could give officers only one piece of advice, I would say, if you've been on the job longer than three years (and depending on what you've been through), you damn well better have a counselor and you damn well better talk to them openly, honestly, and regularly. That's something I wish I had known much earlier in my career, because I needed counseling and I waited a little too long to get it since cops are supposed to be strong. Counseling is for crybabies and washouts who can't hack it, right? How are you going to be ultra macho if you have to talk about weakling bullshit like feelings? Let me tell you, that kind of thinking is poison, and it leads to bad cops, and sometimes, dead cops. It sounds morbid, but, considering that officer deaths from suicide are double what line-of-duty deaths are, regular counseling should be mandatory.[1] When I finally recognized my need and utilized my counselor, they helped tremendously. They helped me start to heal from all the things that I couldn't admit were damaging me so deeply.

This stuff piles up so quickly, and it's impossible not to feel some regret at times. Or is reluctance a better word? I got asked once, "If you knew then what you know now, would you still have wanted to be a cop?" I joined the police department when I was maybe twenty-four, twenty-five years old, and, like most men in their early twenties, I thought, "I can handle anything. It's fine. I got this. Whatever I see won't bother me. I've seen all the gory movies, so that's all the training I need to handle it. What do these bad guys have on Freddy Krueger or Michael Fucking Myers?" This wasn't just a dumb young man being naive; this was how society had taught me to think about being a police officer. *You're tough, so you've got this. Are you a boy or a man?* I wish someone had pulled me aside and told me how it really was; it wouldn't have removed my sense of duty or desire to keep my community safe, but maybe I could have prepared for it. I could have taken some steps to safeguard my mental and emotional well-being.

Police agencies, like anywhere else, recruit or hire when they're short-staffed. There's a need to fill, so they don't want to tell you anything that might douse your interest. They want good candidates to come sign up and get started right away. They're not going to tell you, "Okay, just so you know, in a couple of years you're gonna be pretty fucked up. This job will traumatize the shit out of you, but we really need you to ignore all that so you can start handling calls."

Many of these places don't have the resources to cover the mental health problem. There's what's known as the Employee Assistance Program (EAP), which, if you don't know, offers help to resolve personal problems that negatively impact your work performance—stuff like alcoholism, drug addiction, relationship issues, legal issues, and traumatic events like workplace violence. Sounds great, huh? One-stop shopping for all your mental health needs, like getting your hair cut by your proctologist. Nothing against EAPs, because something is better than nothing and they likely do help some people, but they're unfocused, inefficient, and insufficient. If you're in a crisis, they hand you a pamphlet and tell you "good luck." "We'll give you some time off to get your shit together, but just know, you're really putting us out. Someone has to take over your caseload and we're already spread thin enough. So, hurry back." It's a get-well-soon card with a countdown timer.

Some larger agencies have the financial resources to employ a psychologist on staff who's dedicated to talking to officers, but in midsize and smaller agencies, there's no such thing. At the very least, across the board, there needs to be a contracted, qualified psychologist or counselor—someone who can step in whenever a critical incident occurs or when there's an officer who's showing signs of being in some sort of mental health dilemma, who can say, "Hey, this officer needs help. I'm going to meet with him." You know, instead of just handing out pamphlets like it's an inconvenience. At least act like you care. Yes, plugging holes in the dam is expensive, but so are funerals.

When your help doesn't help, your outlook shifts. You repress and you ignore as you adapt to this new paradigm that things aren't going to improve.

The department assigned me to spend eight hours a day investigating sex crimes involving children, and that's not including the time I spent on middle-of-the-night callouts. I'd already been traumatized by patrol work, but this was an entirely different plane of darkness. Even when my shift was over, no matter what I did, I couldn't escape the details and circumstances of each horrible case, and they just kept repeating over and over, eating away at my mind. When it comes to horror of that nature, there's nowhere to set it down.

I once had to sit across from a sex offender in an interrogation room and, in order to build a rapport in pursuit of a confession, I had to pretend I knew what it's like to be attracted to young children. All the while, I imagined beating him to death right there at the table. Eventually, I got him to confess that he raped his twelve-year-old daughter, recorded it, and sold it to other sex offenders on the internet.

My daughter was eleven years old when I investigated that case.

How can someone be capable of such pure evil? Why would they choose to direct it at anyone, let alone a child? Why are we always too late to rescue them? Why didn't someone help them a week earlier, or an hour, or even *a minute* sooner? Why do people have kids if they're simply going to neglect or abuse them? Then you start figuring out the answers to those questions, and your sadness turns to rage.

Those poor kids—some of them babies—and their stolen innocence bore down on me like the weight of the sea.

I had experienced so much secondary trauma in my career, but it was so gradual I didn't realize it was happening until it was almost too late. I began abusing my sick leave, calling in time after time after time. There were some days where it was all I could do to get out of bed in the morning and, by 9 a.m., I was exhausted and just wanted to go back to sleep. I was already divorced, and my relationships with my daughter, friends, and family were starting to dwindle. I pushed everyone away and retreated into my own secluded world of pain. I was miserably depressed and anxious, and it eventually began to affect how I did my job.

After a squabble with my supervisor about my diminishing performance, I finally admitted that I was struggling mentally and emotionally. It was one of the lowest times of my life. If you imagine "rock bottom," then fifty feet of shit beneath that, that was me. Everyone has their low points but, to me, this one seemed impossible to overcome. All of the stress, trauma, grief, and heartache from my professional and personal life had culminated in this moment. The hundreds of sex crime cases involving children, the child pornography cases, the rapes, the murders, the dead bodies, the battered wives, along with one failed relationship after another, completely did me in. I had no energy, no spirit.

There was just a shadow of my former self in a zombielike state going through the motions, hoping no one would notice.

And it broke me.

I suffered a mental breakdown.

In front of a sergeant, a staff sergeant, and a lieutenant, I wept out all the hate and bile that had been building inside me for years. Humiliation doesn't even begin to describe what I felt.

My administrators, in their infinite wisdom, acknowledged that firing me at that point would have put them in a precarious situation. I would have been able to file a claim against the city for a violation of the Americans with Disabilities Act, considering the severe mental and emotional distress I was experiencing. They placed me on leave in accordance with the Family and Medical Leave Act (FMLA). It wasn't out of compassion that my department gave me that time; it was out of reluctance and a desire to avoid liability. I was told to go home and wait for a call from my supervisor. So I went.

After sitting at home and staring at the wall for a while, I heard a knock at my door, which turned out to be a lieutenant and a captain from the department. They gave me a copy of all the administrative paperwork that indicated I was to be on leave pursuant to the FMLA. I was instructed to report to a psychiatrist for a fit-for-duty evaluation. My lieutenant handed me an EAP pamphlet and said, "Good luck." They left and I sat in silence, wondering if this was the end of my law enforcement career. I'd never felt so alone. At this point, I'd been working for the Twin Falls Police Department for eleven years. I was good at my job. I was considered a rising star at one point. I'd been awarded a medal for bravery, two medals for meritorious service, a unit citation medal, and several letters of commendation. Yet the cold, indifferent demeanor of my supervisors led me to believe that none of the good I'd done over the years mattered and, because I was now showing vulnerability, I was longer an asset to the department.

You know that scene in *Toy Story 2* where the kid looks at his favorite toy cowboy and says in a scary monotone, "You're broken. I don't want to play with you anymore," and then drops him on the ground? That was me—dropped.

I was on leave for three months. I received a few calls from some fellow officers and detectives in the department checking in to see how I was doing. Unsurprisingly (why the hell is this unsurprising?!), no calls came from anyone above the rank of sergeant. I knew then what my place was in the eyes of the department.

I was expendable, and, if I was expendable, so was everyone else who worked there.

The emotions rolled on and on, but the main one I felt on repeat was anger.

When I couldn't take the emotional toll anymore, I looked up and there was that stupid pamphlet. Good luck.

The alternatives to reaching out were grim, so I gathered myself and decided to call the hotline number. I picked up my phone and this is how it went:

Hotline: "...Hello?"

Nate Silvester: "Hello there."

H: "..."

NS: "Sorry, I'm not sure I have the right number. Did I wake you up?"

H: "Can I help you?"

NS: "Uh, hope so. Is this the place on the pamphlet...the

Employee Assistance Program?"

H: "Name?"

NS: "It's Nate. Nate Silvester."

H: "S-y-l?"

NS: "S-i-l."

H: "..."

NS: "I'm looking for a counselor."

H: "..."

NS: "I need counseling."

H: "..."

NS: "I'm a police officer."

H: "Just find one in your area and ask if they accept EAP and they'll take care of it."

N: "..."

Click.

It couldn't have been a more humiliating process. I can tell you that most cops in that situation would have said, "Fuck it," and gone straight to the bar to wash that shit away. The operator sounded like he was still in his teens, and I'd clearly woken him up based on his groggy voice and glaring apathy.

Remember, this is me reaching out for help. I wanted to throw the phone. I wanted to go find that hotline asshole and pound him while I screamed, "Don't you understand the kind of shit I've got on the backburner here? Don't you realize how much I don't want to ask for help, but I did? Don't you know how many of us are dying *right now* because no one's listening?"

Long after that call ended, I was still sitting there with my phone in my hand. I took a hard look at myself and decided I'd push on a little more. One step in front of the other. What could it hurt to try, if only for another day?

It took a while, but I finally did track down a counselor and get the assistance I needed. The healing process wasn't easy, but it worked. I met with a professional who was qualified and engaged, and I was able to get that darkness out of its compartment and out in the open.

Consulting a counselor was easily the best choice I've made in my entire career. If only more officers understood this. As I mentioned before, there is a stigma attached to an officer getting therapy. That stigma starts with resigning yourself to the cold, hard fact that you couldn't handle the pressure on your own. The job got to you. You weren't hard enough. Most police officers have this mentality, but we're all human beings, susceptible to sadness and despair like everyone else. However, you have to hide that away somewhere, because if anyone notices, you might get pulled off the street or away from your desk and reassigned to "light duty."

Most cops are alphas: they want to be in the fight, on the front line. Remember, many officers' sense of identity is grounded in police work, so being pulled out of the fight is a huge hit to morale and self-worth. In order to avoid that, they suppress, deflect, and avoid. Then they begin to withdraw. They pull away from co-workers, friends, and loved ones to prevent any of them from seeing through the facade of a tough, hardened warrior to discover a vulnerable human being who's at the end of his emotional rope.

Now, I'm not suggesting that officers be required to sit in a sharing circle every week and emotionally vomit all over the other participants. In fact, I think any type of group therapy for police is a waste of time, and encourages individuals to say whatever they think will end the session the fastest. I'm not suggesting we need "softer" and "gentler" souls wearing the uniform; I'm very much a proponent of violence and aggressiveness on the part of officers when the circumstances call for it. I'm saying there needs to be some balance in the life of someone who only sees the shitty side of people for twelve hours a day, especially when that shitty side includes exploiting and abusing the innocent. Officers need to free themselves of the stigma that prohibits them from taking advantage of the cathartic and therapeutic value of counseling. It's not weakness to admit you're struggling. Considering the stats mentioned above regarding officer suicide, I'm certain your wife, husband, son, daughter, mother, or father would much rather you swallow your pride and get help so you can be an engaged and loving family man or woman during your time spent with them.

CHAPTER THREE
FACTORY ISSUE

Let's say you're in the market for a new car, and you just so happen to have, oh, a hundred grand to spend on it. You look around a bit and settle on a brand-new Porsche 911 Turbo (it might not be your cup of tea, but work with me here for a second). This thing hauls ass, comes with all the bells and whistles, and looks great on the streets. Whatever might come up while you're driving around, this car can handle it. You dumped a ton of money into this thing, so you'd probably ensure it's taken care of, right?

Except you don't. Against all sense and logic, you do the exact opposite. You redline it at every opportunity, tear around corners, stomp on the brakes, and nail every pothole like you're scoring extra points. You don't change the oil—in fact, you don't do any service at all. You keep it fueled, though, because how else is it going to do what you want? But even when you're not behind the wheel, you pull the parking brake and keep a brick on the accelerator so those RPMs don't dip for a second.

So what happens when that expensive engine starts smoking, the gaskets are shot, and those brakes grind and squeal? Naturally, you'd send it off for repairs, because you're already in this a hundred grand. You'd protect your investment. Except you don't.

Instead, you park it in the garage so it's off the street for a while, but you tell it, "Don't forget your brick!" You come back in a few days, fully expecting that car to be fresh-off-the-lot perfect. So what happens when it clanks and clunks and stalls out?

You act shocked and fire it, of course.

It costs roughly $100,000 to train a police officer over the course of many, many weeks. Some career cops easily surpass five thousand training hours before retirement, and all of that adds up. Factor costs for this level of qualification, and investment starts to get astronomical. And yes, those are taxpayer dollars paying for it. Is it money well spent? Well, yes and no.

What the administrators are trying to create, just like automotive companies, are machines. They want the process streamlined and the bugs squashed so that the next fleet of Lawbot 8000s roll out in chromed perfection. And it's not because of public safety; it's because they help sell an image.

There's something that happens on the climb into the hierarchy of the agency, in those upper echelons of supervisory and administrative work. Something happens along the way where the bosses lose sight—at least in my opinion—of the front-line people, like the patrol officers and the detectives, and the work that we're doing way down here at ground level. They become political, and they become self-serving. And people at the administrative level are much more concerned with their reputations and their images in the eyes of the general public than they are about caring for their employees (i.e. their rather expensive investments). It's a game built around who's up for re-election, and who has whose back behind closed doors.

And it's shady as fuck.

I'd never done police work before 2006, but I picked it up fairly easily (not machine-easy, but easier than most). It was something that I enjoyed doing, so I took time and studied it on my own. I really focused on the job and excelled through the field training phase, which took sixteen weeks. I had an accelerated final phase because they felt that I was ready to go out on my own.

I felt attuned to the job and wanted to do my very best. My mind was always on work and how I could improve. I started to notice things—inefficiencies, redundancies, and unnecessary procedures within our department. I voiced my concerns and my opinions about those things, and most of the time, they fell on deaf ears. But when it comes to things I feel are important and need to change, I'm not the type to let it go. And administration doesn't like that. When they hire an officer, they want you to just fall in line and do as you're told. Don't rock the boat or make any waves; do not question your programming. I wasn't being insubordinate or disrupting the chain of command by rightfully pointing out areas that could be improved in an occupation I cared about.

Everyone has their shitty boss stories, but chances are, if you've ever sought to improve the workplace, your boss or manager still appreciated your initiative. But when I was told, "We're not going to change that because this is the way we've always done it," even though the system no longer worked, I had a hard time with that. Then I got labeled by the same people I was trying to help as some kind of "wild card" that needed to be controlled and observed and scrutinized and disciplined. I was a malfunctioning unit, not for failing to perform my assigned functions, but for not turning a blind eye to obvious shortcomings in the system.

The most frustrating thing about it was the absence of empathy or concern from the administrators. It was very confusing because, once upon a time, they were in my position—meaning they were once front-line patrol officers—so they at least had some experience with actual police work before moving into the big leagues. They weren't always sitting behind a desk, scepter in hand, making administrative decisions from on high. But somewhere along the line, they either completely forgot what it was like or just decided not to care anymore, because, again, it became more about their image and how they looked in the view of the public.

And if Officer Upstart is going to balk at misguided commands, then we might as well just cut him loose and hire somebody else who won't question the questionable.

But don't worry, another one will come down the production line. Plenty more where that came from. These new Lawbot 9000s accept every line of command input, maintain core temperature integrity under inhuman conditions, never discharge their firearms under any circumstances, power down between shifts, and require absolutely no upkeep or upgrading.

The hell of it is, as much as the admins want machines, that's exactly what the public doesn't want. They don't want Robocop to pull them over and cite municipal violation codes in some monotone voice while they freeze for a retinal scan.

"License. Registration. Proof of insurance. Remain stationary. Detecting levels of drug and/or alcohol use. Citizen, you are under arrest."

An interaction like that is uncomfortable. It's a shitty experience and it leaves a bad taste in your mouth. Even worse, you might assume that's how all cops are. If you go to the DMV and get treated like a nuisance, you're going to think that's just how DMVs operate.

I've pulled people over, and I've been pulled over myself. Even if I wind up with a citation, I recognize that a little humanity from a cop goes a long way.

"Hey, how are you doing today? You know, you were going a little fast back there. Not the crime of the century. Can I see your information? We've had a lot of wrecks on this road and I'm just trying to get people to slow down."

Compassion should play a role in police work. I understand that people have to be held accountable for the crimes that they commit, and it's our duty to enforce laws, but we don't have to be dicks about it. Cops have discretion on certain things, like infractions or misdemeanors not committed in our presence. I'm not talking about serious crimes like felonies, but mistakes where some leeway exists. We can and should cut people breaks. That's our discretion as officers, and we should try to do that as much as we can.

One of the most effective ways to alienate police officers from the general public is to hand out unnecessary citations. The soccer mom who's trying to get her twelve kids to practice on time, and to violin lessons, and to a grocery pick-up, and then back to school for a PTA meeting doesn't deserve a citation for failing to slow from a 45 to a 35 zone—unless it's a habit for her to blow through school zones and hop curbs, obviously. Most of the time, she's just struggling to be a decent parent and get her kids where they need to be, and I don't think that warrants three years of higher insurance premiums after receiving a moving violation citation. That's ludicrous.

But you get a lot of officers who say they have this hard and fast rule—like machines do—that if Soccer Mom is more than three miles an hour over, she's busted. More than ten over? She's getting a ticket no matter what. Doesn't matter what her situation is. It doesn't matter how shitty of a day she's having. That's it, end of story. Take your ticket, lawbreaker, and good luck working that into the dinner conversation when you finally do make it home.

Some officers have a reason for being a hard-ass, so they can say that they were consistent in case it ever comes up in court. But I would much rather foster a better relationship between myself and that particular member of the community, not to mention that it may very well be the first interaction of her dozen kids with a member of the police force. Did they learn that the police exist to bully citizens, or that we're human beings capable of offering compassion?

It might be a little exaggerated, but is it a realistic example? You bet your ass it is.

It's not just the struggling soccer mom, either. It's the out-of-towner who isn't familiar with the speed zones or merge lanes. It's the dad heading to a will signing at the hospital. It's the teenager who's late for their only shift because it was too cold for their car to start. It's the guy who just realized his girlfriend's cheating and knows he shouldn't go home yet. It's the young couple finally scraping together enough change from the ag dealership for a date night. It's that separate life you encounter when they're maybe not at their best. This could be their lowest, their most confused, their absolute unluckiest day.

Who were you when you got pulled over?

I've had some bad days. Probably more than my share, truth be told. And I've seen some shit, as the saying goes, as insufficient as that is for describing a constant barrage of people doing truly horrible things. So how do I come off a homicide call and still manage to pull some compassion out of my ass for Soccer Mom? Well, I do it for "good guy" reasons, sure, but there's also a selfishness factor there. The fact of the matter is that treating her like a person is cathartic for me. The burdens we pick up doing this job get heavy over time, and the unfortunate reaction for many cops, when they're faced with hardness, is to become calloused, jaded, angry, and ineffective. What good is it doing to view everyone around you as a criminal? As an enemy? I'm not advocating for naive police officers; obviously, be cautious and safe, because it's a dangerous occupation. But have a heart. And manage your fear.

I've spent a lot of words bagging on previous supervisors and administrators, but I've had some really good ones, too. And, you know, one of the things that they would try to help me understand as a young officer was, "Okay, you pull over this person and you've got some considerations to make. How would you want that person to be treated if that was your mom, your daughter, your brother, your brother-in-law, your father? How would you want another officer to treat one of your loved ones? Think about that the next time you stop someone. If you stop your own mother, how are you going to treat her?" It's a very, very simple concept, but that's what makes it so powerful in building a relationship with the general public.

A few years ago, I was pulled over by a Utah highway patrolman. You guessed it: I was speeding. My fault, totally my fault. But he came to the window and started berating me like a pissed-off dad yelling at his kid for coming home past curfew.

"Do you even realize how fast you were going? Do you know how dangerous that is? This isn't the Daytona 500. What do you have to say for yourself?"

I stared at him for a few seconds, just gobsmacked, and I'm like, "You know, I apologize. I don't have an excuse. Here's my information." He stomped off to his cruiser, then stomped back to my car, wrote me a citation, and said, "Slow down from now on," as he shoved the ticket in my window and took off. And I remember sitting there thinking, "Wow, what a dick."

I decided right there that I never wanted to come across like that. Even if I give someone a ticket, I want to make it the best experience they've ever had with a police officer. Every time. You heard me. And when I approach someone, when I first stop them, I know what they're feeling. They're scared. They're like, "Oh, shit, I should have slowed down" or "I should have had my seatbelt on." It's kind of that sense of going to the principal's office. "How much trouble am I in? What's he going to say?"

So as I approach their vehicle, I have to come prepared and be aware of my tone, my stance, and my overall presence. I don't walk up with my gun in their face, screaming at them to comply and *stay calm!* I greet them with something light like, "Hello there," and immediately their stress level lowers. They think, "Okay, he's not going to yell at me. He's not going to be a total douche." And, like I said, even if I end up citing that person for something, I can still be polite and kind and compassionate. Ticket in hand, I might say, "Listen, I understand that you're late, but this is the second time I've stopped you for this. And so this time I am going to give you a citation. Please slow down. If not for your sake, for your children's sake or other people on the road."

We have to do a better job as officers at fostering that relationship with the public, and it starts with our own communication. I used to teach an Effective Communications class at the academy and with the law enforcement program at the local college. If the students learned nothing else, I wanted them to know that their tone of voice, their volume, their intensity, and even their body language determined how each interaction would go. Nobody likes being stopped by the cops and nobody likes being told what to do. Nobody likes getting a ticket or being handcuffed, but, like I said, it can be done in a non-hostile, non-escalating manner. Getting stopped is no party, but with the right tone, people will be more apt to listen to your instructions, follow commands, and not resist or fight. You're still going to have people who react non-compliantly no matter what, but that's a small percentage.

There's a saying in law enforcement that the suspect dictates how the confrontation goes. He can choose to cooperate or he can choose to resist, but so much of that stems from the cop setting the tone in the first place. An officer makes an impression, and it's up to him whether it's good or bad. It's up to him whether this person feels nervous or anxious or frightened, or if they can be calm and talk to him like he's a human being. It's incumbent upon the officers to do their part in this.

So what about when the situation's already escalated? How do you calm it back down so people (and officers) stop turning into overblown statistics?

When I was with the Twin Falls Police Department, I was a field training officer, and I had this trainee who'd been an officer before and was going through an expedited process because she'd already had experience. Just to clarify, the field training program at the TFPD is a sixteen-week program consisting of four phases, each approximately four weeks long. When an officer graduates from the academy and reports for duty at their agency, they're assigned to their first training officer. The training officer has the discretion to decide how long the trainee will be an observer, meaning the trainer will drive the patrol car and be the primary officer on calls for service, while the trainee simply observes. Most trainers will have their trainee observe for one or two shifts, then throw them in the deep end where it's "sink or swim" time. When the trainee takes the driver's seat in the patrol car, they become the primary officer, navigating their way through the city, responding to radio traffic, writing reports, and engaging with members of the public. In most agencies in Idaho, including the TFPD, officers are "ride-alone," meaning they don't have partners like you see in some of the larger departments in bigger urban areas. A trainee is supposed to respond to calls and regulate their non-directed time as though they were alone, even though the trainer is right there with them.

A trainee in their first phase doesn't know their ass from their elbow when it comes to police work, literally fumbling their way through it. A good trainer will only intervene when there is an officer safety issue, otherwise forcing the trainee to think their way through a call for service. The trainee becomes immersed in the work and must quickly learn what their resources are when handling calls for service. Trainees have a natural instinct to rely on their trainers to hold their hand through complex calls, but most trainers will tell them beforehand to exploit other resources in order to resolve problems. There's no handholding after the trainer leaves, so why start off on the wrong foot?

The expectation is that the trainee will become increasingly competent with each shift, and, by demonstrating their ability to effectively handle calls for service, will graduate to each subsequent phase of the training program. Usually, by the third phase, a trainee is able to handle most calls as a primary officer without much guidance from the trainer.

At the end of each shift, the training officer will complete a DOR (Daily Observation Report) wherein they evaluate the trainee's performance in a number of different categories, ranging from officer safety to communication skills, city orientation, and knowledge of state laws and city ordinances. At the end of each phase, the trainer either makes a recommendation to the supervisor that the trainee moves on to the next phase, or stays in their current phase for remedial training if their performance wasn't satisfactory. So there's a lot riding on how well the trainee performs not only under pressure, but under any circumstance.

Some trainees have an expedited fourth phase if their performance was above average, in which case the trainee's fourth and final phase will only consist of seven shifts. The training officer for the final phase is, ideally, the same officer who oversaw the first phase and can compare the trainee's overall performance and basically close the circle. Once the final phase is complete, the trainer can make a recommendation to the supervisor that the trainee be approved for ride-alone status and become a "real cop" at that point.

So I was the third phase training officer for this trainee, and I'm in the passenger seat while she drives on patrol. She sees a guy zip past and it turns out he's someone we'd dealt with before as a known drug offender in the community. So she stops him and writes him a citation for not wearing his seatbelt, which he wasn't.

Did you catch the detail that he was actually breaking the law and she didn't just stop him because he *might* be up to no good? Because I'd be happy to go back and say it again. She stopped him for breaking the law, not because she *suspected* he was breaking the law.

Anyway, in the meantime, another officer shows up as backup and stands there talking to me while the trainee fills out the citation. We're watching the passengers in the vehicle just to make sure that they're not doing anything suspicious or threatening, which they weren't.

Well, one passenger flicks a cigarette out the window. Our backup officer could not have escalated the situation more perfectly when he suddenly says, "Hey, get out and pick that up before I write you a ticket." Everything was going fine up until that. And the passenger turns around and says something like, "The fuck did you say?" And the backup officer comes back with, "You heard me." They get into this back-and-forth shouting match, bigger and louder by the second. Remember, this has nothing to do with the reason for the traffic stop. I look at my trainee to see how she's reacting. She puts her ticket book down, and she walks over to the window and says, "Danny," (because she'd already gotten his name, like a good cop should), "would you mind just picking up your cigarette butt? It's littering. I could give you a ticket. I don't want to. Would you mind?" Danny's tone shifts instantly and he says, "Yeah, sure. I'm sorry."

She's all but brand new, and this other officer had ten or so years on the job. He comes to me later in the station and says, "Hey, tell your trainee if she ever pulls any bullshit like that again, I'm going to jump in her ass." I pull him to the side and say, "If you ever show up to a traffic stop that I'm on and act that way, I will report you. I don't care who you think you are; don't do that shit again. That could have turned out much worse, thanks to you. Thank God my trainee had a much cooler head than you did over a fucking cigarette butt."

Needless to say, he wasn't pleased. Was he a bad cop? I'll leave that to your judgment. But I will say this: his attitude, his demeanor, and his carriage were all what bad cops have in common. They're the ones who say, "It's not my job to be nice. It's my job to bust criminals." And, just like that, they've stepped down the wrong path. They stick out like sore thumbs, and they should.

It's hard doing what we do but, when it comes down to it, we're just people trying to get through the day, same as you. Some days weigh pretty heavily, but that's no excuse to drag someone else through the shit. A good cop, the kind I'm calling for, maintains compassion despite the hard days.

We're not all assholes, guys, I promise.

CHAPTER FOUR
NEVER OFF DUTY

I got divorced in 2012 while I was still working in law enforcement. And, of course, after the divorce, I was living the life of a single man who liked to go out and socialize. I tried to meet women and go on dates, but the dating pool in Twin Falls, Idaho, is pretty shallow. Eventually, I ran into women who had an ex-boyfriend or an ex-husband who didn't like the fact that their ex-girlfriends or ex-wives were fraternizing with a police officer. And every one of these guys seemed to know that they could call down to the police department, file a complaint, and essentially turn an officer's life upside down over nothing more than spite or jealousy.

In my experience, for what it's worth, the motivation behind all this was machismo. Ego. They thought, "My ex-wife is now in some sort of courtship with this police officer, and that's emasculating." At least, that's the sense that I got. Otherwise, why would they care? Who cares what your ex-girlfriend or ex-wife (or both) are doing? You're no longer in a relationship. Why should it matter who they date, and how is it any of your business? Obviously, there's still some sort of unhealthy attachment there." And I get it. They still have feelings for her and don't like facing the truth that she's moving on without them, especially when her new interest is fit, confident, and authoritative.

"But, oh, they're moving on with a police officer? A public servant, you say? Well, I can throw a wrench into those gears by calling down to a supervisor and saying, 'Hey, your employee is sleeping with my wife. And he's doing it while he's on duty.'"

There's nothing right or moral about it, but they can fabricate the lie and lodge the complaint, and there are no consequences for them because they're just a concerned citizen reporting a possible problem. You're on shift the next day, utterly oblivious to any potential shitstorm looming above, just trying to get the job done, when the complaint rolls in and the sovereign wheels start grinding around you. See, the shitty reality is that the supervisors and administrators in many departments will take those complaints and run with them, and, before you know it, you get caught in the wheels. Instead of being out on the street, protecting the city, you're on leave. It might be paid or it might not, but they put you on leave pending the outcome of an internal investigation. You go home, and you sit, and you wait.

Then they go through every one of your emails.

If you have a department phone, they go through your phone, and then through your timecards, and through all of your private correspondence, and they try to get as much personal information about you as they can instead of just sticking with the original complaint (did this cop have sex with this woman while on shift?). It would be the easiest thing in the world to just *go ask her*, and, if she denies it, case closed. But no. Everyone else is innocent until proven guilty; for cops, you're assumed guilty until they've finished dissecting you. They do all of this digging into your personal and public life, at least during the time you've spent working for the city. And they tell you they're being so thorough for transparency's sake, and to exonerate you.

Due diligence, right?

I make it a point to try to stay grounded in reality and avoid indulging in victim mentality, but it's hard to ignore the witch-hunt vibe you get when your superiors go to such far-reaching measures to nail one of their own. If you were to sit in on some of the interviews that they do for an internal investigation, you'd see that it's the equivalent of tearing out the floorboards to look for a set of keys. Let me show you what I'm talking about with a personal story, because it sure as hell isn't going to show up in your newsfeed.

The police department does a citizen's academy every year, and I was asked to do a presentation on detective work. The event is a way for local residents to come in and learn about police procedures and get an insider's look at what we do. It's an attempt at transparency. We take them through some role-playing scenarios so they can kind of feel what it's like to do police work themselves.

After I was done with my presentation and the class was over, one of the participants—a woman—approached me and started chatting with me, and we got along great. She eventually sought me out on social media and we became friends. We talked back and forth fairly often and she shared a lot about herself, but the one piece of information she didn't share was that she was married. She made no mention of it, gave me no indication of it. There was no ring on her finger. Her Facebook page had no photos of any men anywhere, and her relationship status wasn't displayed. So, I assumed, naturally (and perhaps a little naively), that she was a single woman who'd approached me first. Well, we had a very brief relationship.

And then, maybe a month or so after I met this woman, her

husband, whom I was entirely unaware of, called in and filed a complaint against me. Did they go ask her about it? Nope. Instead, they came flying at me.

I was immediately put on leave. They did an investigation. I called my attorney and he came down and represented me, and was present for a series of interviews which were conducted by a two-person internal investigative unit. And one lieutenant in particular went down this line of questioning:

-Did you ever spend time talking to her on duty?

-Did you ever spend time calling or texting her on duty?

-Did you ever go see her while you were on duty?

-Did you have sex with her while you were on duty?

Let me be clear: as far as any sexual stuff, none of that ever happened while I was on duty. Yes, there was some occasional correspondence back and forth while I was working, but who doesn't have that? I mean, officers spend time talking to their wives or girlfriends all the time when they're on duty. Name a job where that doesn't take place. But when I answered no to all the pertinent questions, the lieutenant asked:

"Okay, well, how about off duty?"

And my attorney cut in and said, "No, no, no, no. Time out, time out. What Officer Silvester does in his time off—especially in the bedroom—when he's not being paid by the city, is none of your business."

Now, what a lot of people don't realize is that, before conducting an internal investigative interview of a public servant, the administration reads that employee what's called Garrity Rights, which come from the case of *Garrity v. New Jersey* from 1967. In it, the officer in question, Edward Garrity, was compelled to answer incriminating questions about himself and his fellow officers and was subsequently fired for doing so. The men appealed to and were upheld by the state supreme court, which ruled that "the option to lose their means of livelihood or pay the penalty of self-incrimination is the antithesis of free choice to speak or to remain silent."

The Garrity rule of today, on the other hand, is essentially a warning that says you're being compelled to answer these questions, and, if you refuse to answer them or if you don't answer truthfully (in the interviewers' minds), you can face further discipline, up to and including termination. And they're dead serious about it. Nonpublic workers would just be read the applicable excerpt from their company policy manual and that would be that. A public servant interview is an entirely different circumstance with additional expectations, responsibilities, and so forth. You are compelled to answer *anything* that comes across the table.

From the 2020 Idaho Policing Policy Manual (IPPM) under the section for Administrative Investigations (emphasis added):

> Administrative investigations are used to document information, determine whether an employee violated agency policy, identify possible disciplinary actions and assess liability.
>
> In criminal proceedings, people are protected by the 5th Amendment from making incriminating statements, **but that does not extend to the administrative investigation**. For any employee subject to discipline, the administrative investigator should provide a 'Garrity Warning' before an interview. A Garrity Warning instructs the employee that they must be truthful in all answers, and if they are untruthful or refuse to answer, they may be

subject to termination. The employee only needs to acknowledge the warning, not consent to it.

Afterwards, an employee can be compelled to answer questions, or if they refuse, the agency head can place them on suspension and initiate termination proceedings.

Just in case it's not clear, a public employee is compelled to answer questions during an investigative interview, no matter how intrusive or sensitive the questions are because, if the employee refuses to answer, they could be terminated. These rules apply to all public employees, but let's not operate under the assumption that all fields are equal here. You don't see footage vilifying teachers on a national level, and you don't see bricks getting thrown at paramedics in the street. When it comes to cops, it's a new level of unreasonable expectation.

When's the last time you were put in an awkward situation like this because some asshole with a phone got jealous?

Unfortunately, this process is technically legal because officers are beholden to the taxpayers (just like any public employee); but should administrators acquiesce to the demands of every taxpayer complaint? Does this seem just to you? What makes them believe they are entitled to know what happens in my bedroom?

Kinda hard to raise a fuss about it when your job is on the line. Your instinct is to comply in order to save your career. If I balk at that question and say, "I'm not comfortable talking about this, and I don't see how it's any of your business or how it's pertinent to the complaint being investigated," then I'm reminded that my job is at stake. That sure as shit doesn't sound like the America I believe in. It sounds like authoritarianism, it sounds like dictatorship, and it needs to change. I don't make it a habit to knowingly sleep with married women, and I didn't know this one was. This woman clearly had some ulterior motive to misrepresent herself in order to have sex with me, then divulge all of it to her husband. I mean, kudos to her for coming clean and telling him the truth, but why did I get dragged into her sick little game and nearly lose my job over it? What's even more perplexing is: why did my administrators play along with it?

When my attorney finished his objection about prying into my intimate life, the lieutenant responded, "I am ordering Officer Silvester to answer the question or he'll be fired."

My attorney replied, "I want it clear that he's answering these questions under objection," which elicited zero reaction from the lieutenant.

So, under direct threat of losing my job, I answered the question. I said, "Yeah, we slept together while I was off duty. I didn't know she was married. Talk to her about that."

Again, zero reaction from the interrogators. I received the silent treatment while they shuffled papers around. In summary of the investigation, they gave me a Letter of Counseling, which is an official way of saying, "You didn't do anything wrong but we need to make it look like we disciplined you, and, although we didn't catch you this time, we will in the future."

There are three possible rulings to any internal investigation:

1. Exonerated (the accused is proven innocent).

2. Substantiated (the accusation was found to be valid and the accused will undergo discipline).

3. Unsubstantiated (there was insufficient evidence to either prove or disprove the accusation). This outcome carries a heavy sense of, "You got away with it...for now." It's the one I received, along with a very cold admonition to keep my personal life

unsullied and not bring the department to disrepute.

Ever had sex while not working? Ever had it put your job at risk? No? Just me then...

The fact of the matter is that, for a cop, there's no such thing as "off the clock." There's no such thing as personal time. Here's another excerpt from the IPPM on Personal Internet/Online Communication:

> As an employee of this agency, your conduct both on and off duty must meet a high standard. This includes, but is not limited to, conduct related to materials posted on the internet or disseminated electronically including email, social media, instant messaging, blogs, forums, video and file-sharing sites.
>
> You should not maintain, or permit to be maintained, internet or other digital content that:
> • Could reasonably be interpreted to express the opinions of this agency. You may comment on a subject of general interest and of value and concern to the public provided that, in doing so, you do not identify yourself as a member of this agency or otherwise suggest or imply that the views expressed are those of this agency.
> • Has both a reference to you being affiliated with this agency and contains content that is unprofessional, unbecoming or illegal, such as lewd sexual conduct, excessive alcohol consumption or similar behaviors. You are reminded that courts

may scrutinize the credibility of a witness from sources like the internet.

• Could be reasonably interpreted as having an adverse effect upon agency morale, discipline and operation, safety of staff or perception of the public.

But what's your reaction to reading those lines? If they're starting to raise some red flags in your mind, you're beginning to see the inherent issues.

Cops are held to a higher standard. I get that. We should be. But if you apply those bullet points to any TikTok, Instagram, Facebook, or YouTube video where you see a cop in his or her uniform attempting to humanize the badge, most, if not all of them, are in accordance with this particular policy, which is similar to most agencies' policies regarding social media. Yet, officers are being fired over their videos because some liberal activist is offended by them.

If I'm off the clock, hanging out at home in jeans and a t-shirt, not one person in the world has any right to monitor what I'm doing. Plain and simple. If I'm hanging out with friends, maybe at a party, and decide to tell (or listen to) a joke, it's not the in the public's interest to be informed of the joke's content or my subsequent reaction to it. I'm not advocating for the right to spew off-color jokes in my spare time if I feel like it.

I don't have to. That's already covered in the fucking Constitution.

Except when you're a cop, apparently. Police officers have to maintain hyper-vigilance both on and off the job, but the hyper-vigilance off the job isn't about keeping an eye out for danger or crime; it's about covering your own ass 24/7 in the likelihood that someone's recording, someone's monitoring, someone has a bone to pick, someone has a friend's uncle's plumber's nephew who has beef with any cop, for any reason, and will (not might) wake up one day and decide to take it out on you. Or me. Or any of the nearly 800,000 officers with a bullseye on their backs.

When it comes to the point where you can't relax in your own home or with your friends when you're out to dinner, that's where the intrusiveness has crossed the line. It will eventually become detrimental to your emotional and psychological wellbeing, because there's nowhere to be at ease so you can unwind and recuperate. Any stressed-out parents who haven't had a break from their kids in years and kind of want to implode? I think we're speaking the same language here.

Here's another example. Back in 2007 or so, I had a lieutenant who was big into jiu-jitsu, and he wanted officers to start training in it because he felt it helped with the job (he was 100% correct). He set it up so that every Tuesday and Friday, anybody who wanted to come "roll" was welcome. No obligation to go, since it was taking place outside of shift hours and no one was getting paid to be there. I showed up, along with a few other officers, pretty consistently. Now, it's jiu-jitsu, right? It's a physical contact sport. Anybody who's done it knows that injuries, while not terribly common, do happen occasionally, even when you're being careful. Heel hooks, shoulder locks, rear naked chokes, kneebars. It's not ping-pong.

Well, we had one guy who, for whatever reason, got hurt almost every time he came. We had to take him to the ER a couple of times for a broken wrist or a dislocated thumb. It was always something. When this happens to a cop, he gets put on light duty (non-patrol). You have to be physically able to do the job which, if you're in a cast, you can't. So some administrators started to raise some eyebrows.

They said, "What's causing all the need for light duty here?"

It's a fair question to ask, for sure, especially because it just kept happening to this one particular cop over and over. It may have appeared intentional to some, but one or two questions would have solved that case damn quick. Instead, they outlawed the class. No more jiu-jitsu for anyone, injured or otherwise. That thing you chose to do with your free time that was also helping make you a better cop? Gone.

We were poor growing up, but my friend had a trampoline we used to jump around on. It was a blast—until one day, the little brother climbed on and got bounced a little too hard, and ended up with bonk on his head. Out came my friend's mom, who naturally overreacted and decreed that no one was allowed to get on the trampoline ever again.

Isn't it fucked up that the comparison is so easily drawn between an overreacting mother and these supposedly vaunted officials? We—officers of the law—got *grounded* from jiu-jitsu.

At the Twin Falls Police Department, I had a lot of good coworkers who all got along really well, and we'd sometimes travel to Boise as a group. It was our chance to get out of our jurisdiction, out of our patrol areas, and just be human for a change. As adults do all around the world, we went to bars to have a good time, do some dancing, maybe have some drinks. Nightlife in Boise tends to be much more interesting than in Twin Falls, unsurprisingly, but the real payout is the chance to kick back and blow off steam without keeping a running tally of how many criminals you personally know in your line of sight.

Well, somebody, somewhere along the line, decided to call our supervisor and tattle on us. So in comes a call from one of the top dogs to put the kibosh on these off-duty miscreants who are just trying to take a breather. Mind you, we're not breaking any laws; we're not causing a fuss; we're not even breaking any department policies. We're literally just out at a bar when this supervisor calls to intervene.

"What are you doing traveling to Boise? What business do you have there, outside of your area?"

"We're here to relax as a group of friends. What does it matter?"

"Well, we're just concerned about what that looks like."

"What does it look like?"

"It's just that, if you guys got into a fight, it would reflect poorly on the department."

"Why would we get into a fight? And why should that matter anyway? If we do happen to break the law—not that it's going to happen—the cops here will take of it, right? We're not on the clock, and you're not paying us for the time we're spending here."

"Just be aware that your actions have a direct impact on the department. It looks like you're going out of town in order to hide whatever you're doing."

Well, we were. Not because we were doing anything wrong, but we wanted to be in a place where no one knew we were cops. So we could let our guard down for a few hours and enjoy ourselves. So that some jackass couldn't try and push our buttons or spend the entire night recording us on his phone.

I've had similar interactions with my dad when I was out past curfew or hadn't checked in. You know what the difference is there? They were with my own father, and I was a fucking child, not a fully grown, fully trained, fully responsible adult. Remember, this scolding wasn't just for me as the wayward upstart in the administration's eyes; it was for a group of adults operating outside of their professional capacity for one night.

It's maddening. As I sit here writing this, I'm still seething with anger about it. What kind of egomaniac do you have to be to think you get a say in a person's private life, let alone an entire department's—not only that, but to make up the rules as you go to justify your intrusive mindset? I mean, do you give a single shit about what your doctor does when she's not in the examination room with you? Does it have the slightest bearing on your treatment if she goes dancing with her friends on the weekends?

Of course it doesn't. We, the officers, have been entrusted to police an entire city and ensure that the citizens uphold the law, but we can't be trusted to relax outside of shift hours? What's the true concern here, as far as police administration goes? What's the risk to "the department?"

Well, it's not that we might get cited with battery and charged with a misdemeanor. That's on us as individuals. It's not like the police department gets a bill each month for how many citations their employees received. It's not like anyone from administration has to lift a finger if a cop fucks up in their spare time. If I break the law, it goes on my own permanent record, and I'm the one who has to deal with the court dates and any subsequent penalties, fees, or jail time.

The real risk is how it looks in the eyes of the general public, and how that reflects on whoever's up for re-election. Don't get me wrong, cops shouldn't break the law, but that's a far cry from rolling down the slippery slope that one of us *might*, and therefore must be excessively scrutinized with overwhelming suspicion while we're not at work.

Cops aren't supposed to profile citizens for crimes they haven't committed (we don't), so why can administrators profile their officers the exact same way?

Yes, I'm fully aware that I'm a trained law enforcer, capable of meeting force with greater force and using my department-sanctioned skills to drop an aggressor at a moment's notice. I'm a walking arsenal, because I have to be. I have to keep that—and my temper—in check at the bar, but you know where else I have to keep it in check? Everywhere else. Everywhere. Every single traffic stop, investigation, pat-down, domestic dispute, noise ordinance violation, gas station interaction, grocery trip, school event, crosswalk, Home Depot parking lot, at a picnic, or the library, a restaurant, the gym…even my own backyard. Imagine enjoying a cookout with your family and suddenly getting a phone call from the police department admin asking if you happen to be breaking any laws. Would you be confused? Would you feel like they were overstepping their bounds? And if it happened all the time, would you be angry? Maybe you'd want to scream into your phone: "It's none of your fucking business what I'm doing in my home!"

The expectation of perfection is idiotic. On top of that, it's problematic. I get that we're accountable to the city and its citizens for our actions, but that doesn't mean the citizens are always right. It doesn't mean they know more about being cops than we do. Let's say, for example, I'm at that bar and some guy gets in my face to make trouble. Out come the phones to record, because they're always present eventually. I get recorded in a situation I'm trying to de-escalate and someone sends that recording to the police department with a note that: "Officer Silvester is out here picking fights at the bar." Then I succeed in calming down this guy who's in my face, the altercation fizzles, and we each go back to whatever was happening before. No harm done, right? That clip of me, and the significant damage it's capable of, is already well on its way to ruining my life. No fight took place, no charges were pressed, nothing happened at all, but the "evidence" is already on record, along with the "valid" complaint from that concerned citizen who only cares about the welfare of the public.

It doesn't matter if you're halfway across the state or halfway around the world, because that's the nature of social media and instant technologies. You could be chilling on a private beach in the Bahamas and somebody's still going to find you.

And, with enough coverage, everybody slips up.

What's it like to be a cop in a restaurant? For most police officers, at least in my experience, there's a kind of consensus that you keep an eye out for people you've dealt with. Maybe arrested for a felony. Maybe tackled during a foot pursuit. You start running down lines of connections, networks between the criminals you've engaged and who might be associated with them in your immediate vicinity. A family member of somebody you cited for a disturbance, or wrote a speeding ticket for, or hauled in on a drug offense. Doesn't matter that the offense was valid or the charge earned. People get upset about those things, and it doesn't take much upsetting before they start looking to retaliate. Some life hacker with a YouTube degree in litigation. Some tweaker who's been stewing behind bars for a few months and cannot wait to get out and act on this grudge he's been nursing. If you're a cop, you're going to piss off a whole lot of people.

So, yeah, when I go into a restaurant, especially if I'm with my family, I have to make sure that there are no present threats. I want to sit in the furthest rear of the restaurant with my back against the wall so nobody can come up behind me. I only want to worry about my 90-degree view, not what's going on outside of my periphery, because that's not optimal safety. I need to see the entrance so I can monitor who comes in the door, what they're carrying, what they might be hiding. I need to see who's going to and from the bathroom, if they're acting strangely, maybe even experiencing a medical emergency. I need to see my escape routes. I look for the nearest exits I can take to get to my car, which will be backed into the parking spot so I can get out of there quickly, if the situation calls for it. How clear is the path to my car?

You see this kind of thing in the movies and cop shows sometimes, and they have that part absolutely right. It's hyper-vigilance, and there is no possibility of relief from it. At some point, someone bearing a grudge is going to act on it. Will it be when I'm taking a piss? When I'm opening the door for my date? When I'm reaching for my wallet to pay the check? What about later when they've followed me home?

Will it be when I'm asleep?

Will they come after my family? Will it be my family first, or me? Please, God, let it be me first so I can deal with it or, if I can't, they can at least have time to get out to safety...

Paranoia indicates fear based on the unknown or the unlikely. What goes through the minds of cops is not paranoia; it's a very real fear of being unprepared for that one split second when it matters most. And it keeps us up at night.

One of the best trainings I've ever attended was called "Emotional Survival for Law Enforcement" by Dr. Kevin Gilmartin. He based the training on the book he wrote by the same name. I actually went to his training twice because it resonated so deeply with me. The gist of what he teaches law enforcement personnel is that you must have an identity outside of law enforcement. Let yourself be a person, not just 100% cop every second of the day. Take on hobbies (if the idea of a cop throwing a frisbee sounds ridiculous, maybe take a step back and figure out why). Foster your relationships with your family and your friends, because being a cop quickly takes over your whole identity. You're going to burn out very quickly and you're going to deal with a lot of emotional and mental trauma that you should have been dealing with all along by going fishing or playing basketball or working out. We get so focused and zoned in on police work that we completely forget about everything else. Some officers take their radios home and listen to the radio traffic while they're sitting, eating dinner, or watching TV, just in case anything exciting happens.

"Maybe they'll need me. Maybe they'll call me during my off time and I can go in and help serve a search warrant or something. Maybe they'll need one extra guy for backup. Maybe I should be there now, just in case."

And that's bad. It really is. It's unhealthy to be that concerned with police work, especially when you're off duty. No one can work that much and not feel the impact.

I joke about this all the time because, when you go to a cop training, even though officers aren't in uniform, they're still in uniform. You can look around and see the khaki BDU pants with the tactical cargo pockets. Everyone's in some kind of black or gray shirt that has an American flag on it, maybe a Punisher skull, or a black hoodie, or a camouflage hat, or some article of clothing that they got from a firearms manufacturing company. And most, if not all, are carrying concealed guns. That's your typical cop in training. I'm not saying there's anything wrong with that, but you can spot a room full of police officers even when they're off duty and out of uniform, when they're supposedly at ease. The persona runs deep, and the lifestyle eventually overtakes everything.

Administration expects that when you're off duty, you're

deactivated at home, doing nothing that might make the department look bad, nothing that might make your supervisor look bad, nothing that might make people question for an instant whether cops are anything less than well-oiled machines.

I can't just pull into a gas station to fuel up my personal car on the weekend, bopping along to some music, and not keep both eyes peeled for danger. Because, if the shit hits the fan and there's a robbery or altercation, I have to be prepared to immediately take action. It's these types of situations that officers are always mentally preparing for. It's called "crisis rehearsal." You play out every possible scenario in your mind and anticipate every possible circumstance and factor to determine how you will react should you happen upon a crime in progress.

I was always told to try and be a good witness first. Obviously, if someone poses a deadly threat to an innocent, it's my duty to act. And the court of public opinion would agree, as long as his skin color is the same as mine.

News flash: public opinion of cops is at an all-time low. The simple fact that you're holding my book right now is evidence that our system and our society are flawed; this book only exists because there's a problem. My voice shouldn't stand out. What I'm saying shouldn't surprise anyone, but it does, because shit is broken.

So, if the administrators want immaculate Lawbots that are all-cop-all-the-time, why send us to trainings where the leading advice of mental health professionals says exactly the opposite? According to administration, hobbies are out because I might sprain a thumb (so long, *CoD*, we've had some good times). Can't go fishing, because I might take a hook to the eye and lessen my effectiveness. Can't play basketball, because someone might record me talking trash with my friends, or I might twist an ankle, or skin my knee, or get winded. God forbid my electrolytes drop between shifts.

That Porsche is idling in the garage, and the engine's cracking. The gaskets are blowing out, the transmission's seizing, and the weight of that brick on the accelerator is getting heavier, and heavier, and heavier.

Off duty my ass. There's no such thing.

Cops are never off duty.

CHAPTER FIVE
COP MYTHS

I served as a deputy marshal assigned to a somewhat rural area in Idaho, and I got snide comments here and there along the lines of, "You think you're a real cop?"

First off, fuck this question and the insinuation behind it. It doesn't matter if you're patrolling Miami Beach or a back alley in St. Louis, and it doesn't matter if you earned your badge at LAPD or NYPD. A cop is a cop is a cop.

Let's get this straight. The person asking this type of question isn't a cop—or won't be for long. It's not a competition to see who has the biggest dick, and you won't catch good cops operating under this assumption that higher crime cities produce better police officers.

But what about the public's perception? If you break the law in a big city, you expect Officer Clegane to step out of his personal tank and crush you under his boot. Tell me I'm wrong. But what about a rural area? Do you assume that the responding officer is untrained in some way? Poor Barney Fife. He's never even drawn his gun and he's just doing his best to keep farmers from getting in bar fights on Saturday afternoons. Where do you suppose that stigma comes from?

The Twin Falls Police Department is a small-to-midsize agency in comparison with places like Houston or Chicago. In the time I was there, we were never fully staffed, and each officer had a heavy call volume. A police officer's primary responsibility is responding to calls for service, so that's what fills most of your time on shift. On a busy night, I might have had twenty-five to thirty calls during a twelve-hour shift. That's a lot of calls. Compare that to, say, Boise PD, where an officer might respond to ten calls during a twelve-hour shift pretty regularly. We were constantly short-staffed (apparently treating your employees like shit has consequences), so that meant I'd handle a heavier workload than most, simply because there was no one else present to do it. We had about seventy sworn officers at the time, but they didn't all work at the same time, and it felt stretched.

Now, when those cops came on shift, they were responsible for the safety of a city. In the case of a night shift, it was five officers to about fifty thousand people. That's a lot. In fact, it's more than a lot. It's herculean.

LAPD is a good measuring stick because they're such a large agency, and they have a lot of area to cover. Their department is comprised of bureaus, offices, divisions, sections, and areas. Take the Rampart Division of the LAPD, for example: they have 330 police personnel that serve 165,000 residents in their area of responsibility.[2] That's one officer for every five hundred people. The Twin Falls Police Department has seventy officers who serve a population of 55,000 people. That's one officer for every 786 people. The call volume that an LAPD officer receives in a night is going to be similar, if not possibly lower, to that of a TFPD officer, just by the numbers.

Being a smaller agency, Twin Falls didn't have separate divisions like LAPD, which has focused divisions like robbery and homicide. We had one detective division that was responsible for all of the crimes that needed further investigation, and cases often involved the likes of grand theft and murder. I served as one of those detectives for several years, and I investigated homicides and robberies. I worked undercover in narcotics; I know what the drug world is like. I investigated sex crimes, so I know what that evil looks like. And everything else in between, whether it was a burglary or a home invasion or a domestic violence issue—I've done all of it.

Crimes are being committed—and police are stopping them—in every city in the US, and there is no such thing as a quality scale for which cities make the best cops.

Similarly, I've heard the assumption that, because I work in Idaho, I only police white people. Or that I have a limited viewpoint because I haven't dealt with certain minority groups. This is a close-minded assumption, and it likewise carries that insinuation that I'm somehow deficient in my job performance.

We don't live in the age of telegraphs and handwritten correspondence. We don't need the Pony Express to bring word of the outside world. We have the news, we have television, we have social media. So I see what's going on in other parts of the country and in other parts of the world. My eyes are not blind to the fact that we're a very diverse country and we have people living in our communities who have different cultures and different beliefs, different religions and different ways of living their lives.

Bellevue and Twin Falls have very large Hispanic populations, and we've seen an influx of Middle Eastern ethnicities in this part of the state recently. We have a refugee program here, and we see people from Turkey and Iraq, as well as other Middle Eastern and Eastern European countries. I don't claim to have an intimate knowledge of their cultures, but I'm aware of the challenges that arise in moving to another country.

For example, in some societies in the Middle East, it's not illegal to beat your wife.

So we get a domestic violence call for an Iraqi couple. Somebody has called the cops because the man put his hands on his wife, so then we show up. And he doesn't know why we're there.

"What are you doing in my house?"

"Well, sir, what you're doing is illegal here. You can't beat your wife."

He's perplexed. "But why is this illegal?"

If I were the daft hillbilly that some people try to make me out to be, I'd obviously feel that this man has threatened me and denigrated my beloved country's laws, and must therefore pay the price. If the media had its way with dictating their reality, I'd open fire on this scumbag and unload twenty rounds into him and (collaterally) his poor wife. *Then* I'd read him his rights.

But I don't do those things. I see that he's confused, but only because someone showed up to tell him he can't do something he, and everyone he's ever known, have done without consequence or repercussion for hundreds of years. In his world, his actions are lawful. Imagine if, oh, I dunno, you had the right to own and use a firearm in protection of your home for the last 230 years, and suddenly someone, oh, I dunno, said you can't have it anymore.

Would you be a little perplexed? I sure would. I might appreciate an understanding tone and some explanation. I might appreciate it to the point that I would listen, comply, and never have an issue like this again. I might.

People have the strangest misconceptions about the police—like what they do, how they act or react—and it gives rise to a lot of disinformation, rumors, and lies. Some of it's fear, some of it's bad luck...some of it's true. So I wanted to address some of the myths surrounding officers in general, because they're just so incredibly off-base.

Quotas

Myth: You get pulled over on the 29th of the month. You were speeding, but only a few miles per hour over. You feel like the cop should have looked the other way. He approaches your car. You explain. He listens. You get a ticket. You curse under your breath that he only gave you the ticket to fill his damn quota for the month.

Truth: There is no such thing as a quota for cops, and you were probably in a school zone. If you're in government work, there are no bonuses. No gift baskets. No set of steak knives. Cops don't win prizes for having the most citations of the week. Quotas would only serve to encourage corruption with officers fabricating probable cause in order to make arrests.

That Being Said: Cops should have personal goals to improve their work efficiency, and all stats get reported to the FBI, which creates the Uniform Crime Reporting (UCR) Program. However, reporting numbers is *not* the same as incentivizing arrests or citations.

Ticket Locks

Myth: Once a cop decides to write a ticket, there's no turning back or avoiding the citation.

Truth: A cop can (if they made a mistake or if new

information comes to light) opt to void the citation hours after it's been written. I'm not going to claim that happens all the time, but there is no such thing as being locked into a ticket on the spot.

<u>That Being Said:</u> Don't lose your shit if you see the officer start writing the ticket. They may or may not change their mind, but blowing up when you see the citation is only going to make things worse for you. Just stay calm. If you want to fight it, do that in court, not the street.

Court No-Shows

<u>Myth:</u> That asshole cop who gave you a speeding ticket is too big of a coward to face you in court. Cops know they're always wrong about the citations they give, so they'll never show up to oppose you. Just go to court, and you'll win every time.

<u>Truth:</u> When someone pleads "not guilty" and a hearing is scheduled, the officer receives a subpoena and is compelled to appear just like any other witness. So, barring some type of emergency or exigency, the officer will be there to testify against you. I testified in every hearing for which the defendant pleaded "not guilty" to the charge. That's an important part of police work. The case isn't over once an arrest is made or a citation is issued. Every defendant has a right to a trial, so my work typically isn't done until the judge or jury renders a verdict—and even then, it depends. I will tell you that most of the time when a defendant pleads "not guilty" to an infraction, they're doing it hoping that the officer won't show up or the prosecutor just doesn't feel like presenting their case that day. You're very unlikely to have

your citation dismissed on the basis that you really, really don't want to pay the fine. The officer and the prosecutor are going to show up prepared, so if you're going to tie up everyone in court that day, you might as well come with a prepared defense.

That Being Said: The same burden of proof that lies with the state in other court cases applies to infractions as well, so if your strategy is to simply sit back and allow the prosecution to prove their case, that is your right.

Cops Hate Cameras

Myth: Cops wish they were invisible to public scrutiny so they could more easily falsely arrest innocents, beat and/ or shoot minorities, and secretly instigate riots on behalf of Antifa.

Truth: Body cams save lives and careers. Cops rely on camera footage to investigate crimes, including accusations of officer misconduct. I can't count how many times I've heard an accusation roll through that a cop did something horrible, only to have the body cam footage or audio recording instantly discredit the accuser. It's happened to me countless times.

That Being Said: You may have seen footage of an officer dealing with someone trying to record them, and the officer orders them to stay back and not interfere with their investigation. This isn't because the officer doesn't want to be recorded; it's an officer safety issue. He or she now has to worry about whether this person holding the camera might present an active threat, which includes trying to distract law enforcement from possible dangers. The officer's attention is now divided between his original investigation and this person holding a cell phone, who could easily pull a gun or a knife and attack the officer while he or she is focused on other things.

Cops Shoot to Kill by Choice

<u>Myth:</u> Cops are expert marksmen who, under duress, can snipe the wings off a fly, and can therefore shoot criminals at any targeted body part they choose. They could easily shoot someone in the leg or arm to wound them, thus simultaneously stopping the crime and saving a life. Cops only shoot to kill because they love willfully killing people. Take their guns away and save lives.

<u>Truth:</u> Man, I don't even know where to start. Anyone who's had firearms experience knows damn well how difficult it is to hit a stationary target at center mass. You've got roughly six-by-six inches in that zone, and it takes substantial practice to make that shot from, say, twenty-five yards, even when you're standing still with utmost focus. What if the target's moving? Now the shot is exponentially harder, but harder still if it's not on a moving track and instead running wildly to escape or attack. You can't anticipate where it's going. Your odds of hitting a hand that's wielding a knife or a foot on a runner are next to nothing. Let's say, for example, I'm the officer who rolls up on the scene with Ma'Khia Bryant, who's brandishing a knife and charging two other women with intent to kill. I draw my gun to eliminate the threat to human lives, but I try to shoot the hand that's waving the knife around. Now I'm shooting rounds downrange that are incredibly unlikely to hit my target. Instead, they're hitting

vehicles. They're hitting people. And now I'm joining her as a danger to society instead of aiming for center mass to stop her before she stabs someone.

<u>That Being Said:</u> The loss of human life is tragic no matter the circumstances, which is why Officer Nicholas Reardon made the *correct* snap decision to end further loss of life, and I salute him for it.

Chokeholds

<u>Myth:</u> Cops don't need to use chokeholds or neck restraints for any reason, and it's about damn time that they've been outlawed by legislation for the greater safety of the populace. What a huge relief that they're now a felony charge.

<u>Truth:</u> They've taken a tremendous tool away from law enforcement, one that not only works incredibly effectively, but that's generally not harmful to the recipient. Find some statistics before you blow your lid. Can chokeholds be lethal? Yes, but look: brain cells are sensitive to oxygen deprivation, but only begin to die after the oxygen supply has been cut off for around five minutes. Unconsciousness happens 8-14 seconds after choking. Upon release, the subject regains consciousness naturally without difficulty in 10-20 seconds. A trained officer knows the proper use of the chokehold and when to release, plain and simple. Regardless, a neck restraint is only used as a warning to a perpetrator. You squeeze, tell them to calm down, and squeeze again if they resist. It only takes one or two squeezes before you've sapped their strength anyway. The only—I repeat, the *only*—need for actual incapacitation from a neck restraint is if the perpetrator can somehow withstand those

warning squeezes, such as someone tripping balls on meth or PCP. For all other altercations, the hold is immensely useful and vastly safer than the media portrays it to be. If we're in the habit of taking effective tools away from trained professionals, it won't be long before cops are out there fighting bad guys with Wiffle bats and kazoos (more on that later).

<u>That Being Said:</u> It might seem like a thin margin for error, but in comparison with how long it takes to pull a trigger, fifteen seconds is a hell of a lot of time. Cops operate in split-second increments during every contact, and neck restraints save far more lives than they end. If you ask me, many cops have become far too reliant on tasers, which carry a greater likelihood of injury to suspects than neck restraints do. If we funnel more funding into police training and teach them hand-to-hand combatives, and the safe and proper application of chokes, we'll see a marked decrease in suspect and officer injuries.

Blue Walls

<u>Myth:</u> Police officers protect their own with a so-called "Blue Wall of Silence." Any cop who breaks the law is automatically shielded from any repercussions by their fellow officers. This allows them to freely act on their homicidal, racist, ultra-violent compulsions without fear of consequence. The Wall prevents everyday US citizens from lodging complaints and securing justice for being wronged by police.

<u>Truth:</u> In case it's not rampantly obvious, one of the overarching themes of what I'm trying to get across is how ready and willing police department leadership is to throw

any cop under the bus for stepping a toe out of line. One call from a citizen is enough to end a career. I've never seen or experienced anything resembling this unlawful barrier for cops. I don't want to come across as naive, but my experience has been that the majority of police officers have enough moral fiber that, if they saw another cop behaving unethically or criminally, they'd report it to their supervisor and the offending officer would suffer the consequences. There is no Blue Wall of Silence as far as I can tell.

That Being Said: I can't say without question that this hasn't happened in the past at some point, but everything I've seen completely refutes its existence. Departments are internally regulated, so if someone at the top is encouraging misbehavior or turning a blind eye toward questionable actions, using their power to force lower-level law enforcement to keep their mouths shut, the concern is feasible. But some of these admins can't wait to fire someone for a TikTok video, so how could they support the lawbreaking of their officers? Police officers experience excessive scrutiny daily, and sweeping misconduct under the rug doesn't align with my experience.

Get Out of Jail Free Card

Myth: Similar to the above myth, but this one involves one cop pulling over an off-duty cop for some infraction, running their identification, and giving a free pass due to professional courtesy. The stopping officer swipes my ID and the computer pops up with a big blue banner across my profile that says, "He's a cop; he's void of consequence."

Truth: The off-duty cop is held to the same standard as

everyone else. If anything, they'll incur a heavier fine because they should know better. There is no freebie feature to being a police officer. We enforce laws, so how is it fair if we don't police ourselves as well? The computer displays necessary information, like any current warrants or infractions, but it doesn't report employment status for anyone.

That Being Said: I can't imagine trying to weasel out of a ticket by flashing my badge. It's pathetic. What a phenomenal way to disrespect the occupation and put that other cop in an unnecessarily awkward position of giving you a citation anyway. Do us both a favor and keep your job to yourself.

The Crazies

Myth: Cops should properly identify the mental health status of everyone they encounter during a crisis and alter their actions accordingly. If the situation goes south, it's the fault of the police officers at the scene for failing to properly de-escalate the situation. Couldn't they see the man had a condition?!

Truth: Cops do this out of sheer necessity, and it happens way more often than you might think. Altercations with the mentally ill aren't always combative, and we have training to approach people with mental health issues, but circumstances can change in an instant. You can't ask a social worker to respond to someone in crisis when he's naked and threatening others with a knife. The officers are there to deal with the threat of violence, and that's no time for a therapy session. When someone is agitated, violent, and not listening to anybody, we're there to restrain, control, and transport if need be. Therapy comes later. Being mentally ill doesn't make this guy any less capable of harming himself or others with that knife, and it's a little shortsighted to assume so.

That Being Said: People want one-stop-shopping when it comes to first responders. It would be amazing to have a fully trained police officer with a psychiatric license and a social work degree, but those are separate fields. Some officers do have degrees in social work, counseling, or criminal justice, but they're the exception, not the rule. We have loads of training and there's always room for more, but when shit hits the fan, scene safety is paramount; singing "Kumbaya" in group therapy comes later. That doesn't make us Neanderthals just looking for an excuse to club someone into submission. We genuinely care about the safety of everyone involved.

Schadenfreude

Myth: Cops get off on citing people for petty shit. They thrive on the misery of others.

Truth: Tickets blow. I've already talked about not wanting to increase someone's insurance premiums for three years, but that's not my only consideration. There are those motorists that will only learn if they take a hit to their pocketbook and a blemish on their driving record. There are very few cops who find gratification in ruining people's day with a citation. If you're one of them and you're reading this, do better.

That Being Said: I've had some satisfying busts. It feels

good to nab a criminal and get a little rush of justice to the head. However, it's not justice to throw citations at people who could easily have been given a warning and sent on their way. Nut up, go find a real criminal, and quit bullying people.

Mouthiness

Myth: Flipping off a cop can get you arrested. Saying "Fuck you, pig!" to a cop can get you arrested. Driving past a cop while oinking and shouting, "I SMELL BACON!" can get you arrested. Examples *ad nauseam* because this type of treatment has been around forever.

Truth: The First Amendment exists. Anything spoken or otherwise communicated toward a cop is covered by your freedom of speech (unless you're undergoing an internal police investigation while employed by the department, mind you, in which case it disappears in a puff), and there are no ramifications to expressing yourself toward an officer. Get creative, though, because we've heard it all before.

That Being Said: Don't be a douche. That cop doesn't deserve that kind of treatment. They've had a long, long day, and their situation sucks, and they get enough bullshit from real criminals. Bear in mind that you can say what you want, but if the officer considers your actions or speech to be threatening in any way, you'll be hearing lots more about your rights soon after.

Four Lefts

Myth: A cop is behind you in traffic, but they haven't pulled you over. You drive for a ways, but they're still behind you.

You make a left turn down some side street. The cop goes left as well, right behind you now. Nervously, you wonder why they're there and make another left turn at the next available street. The cop is still there in your rearview. Suddenly, you remember your uncle's voice granting this sage piece of advice: "Cops can't follow you for more than three turns. As soon as you make a fourth turn, the cops have to leave you alone." Ready to break the standoff, you flick on your left-turn signal, signaling the cop's doom and your easy victory as you turn into someone's driveway and see the cop pass by in defeat.

Truth: You stop in the driveway and the cop asks for your license and registration. You've been driving suspiciously for a few turns and the cop has legitimate concern that you may be in some kind of personal emergency or involved in criminal activity. Not to mention, you were weaving all over the place while watching your rearview mirror instead of focusing on the road. Right away, you check several boxes for suspicious behavior, including likely intoxication and drug use. And you're just driving weird. Who drives like that?

That Being Said: It doesn't matter if you turn four times or four hundred times; if a cop has reason to suspect you for something, there are no magic actions you can take to avoid them.

Personal Use

Myth: Cops can and will use department resources to stalk whoever they want and look into their private lives. If you plan on dating a police officer, be assured they've already learned everything about you with their vast government spy technologies, accessed through your license plate number.

Truth: We can't do this; it's illegal and a gross misuse of department resources. It's actually a felony. If we want to cyberstalk someone, we have to do it the old-fashioned way like everyone else and just use Facebook or Google. The oft-used line in Hollywood, "I got a buddy down at the station who owes me a favor," is entirely false.

That Being Said: That's it. It doesn't happen. There are plenty of other forces at work to bring our careers to a screeching halt. We're not about to throw it all away to get a peek at the criminal history of our latest love interest.

I'm gonna break from the list to cover this last myth, which is every cop-hater's favorite topic: Bad Apples. If you don't know the idiom, it goes: "One bad apple spoils the bunch." The implication here is that one bad apple (bad cop) makes all the other apples (cops as a whole) rotten. Where there's one bad thing, there might be more. So you find that bad apple and snatch it away from the rest, hoping that its rot didn't corrupt any of the others, but you can't fully guarantee that, so you might need to throw out the entire harvest, just in case. Defund the apples.

Chris Rock had a stand-up bit that went viral last year where (speaking about the police) he said, "Bad apple? That's a lovely name for 'murderer.'" He goes on to say, "Some jobs can't have bad apples. [...] Like pilots. American Airlines can't be like, 'Most of our pilots like to land. We just got a few bad apples that like to crash into mountains. Please bear with us.'"[3]

Well, Mr. Rock, let me say that commercial pilots don't typically have their passengers trying to fight with them or kill them as they're piloting the plane. And you can have bad apples with commercial pilots. I mean, it's not unheard of. There are pilots who have flown drunk, or high, or whatever, but nobody really cares to hear about that stuff. It's not reported on. What gets reported is the instant an officer discharges a firearm, and how the entire nation suddenly shows up to weigh in. And they're looking for dirt. They're looking for wrongdoing. They're looking for hesitation, lack of hesitation. They're scrutinizing every frame of action or inaction to find the error. To find that rogue cop. However, this isn't really about bad apples. The "bad apples" thing is just a narrative. This is about behavior and consequences for that behavior.

"Oh, it was some white guy in his thirties? Meh. Oh, another guy was Pakistani? Meh. Hispanic? Meh. But keep me posted the moment there's any white-on-Black involvement."

Is Chris Rock trying to tell me that if a white airline pilot were being attacked mid-flight by a Black passenger that physical force wouldn't be used to eliminate that threat? I certainly hope it would, for the sake of the other innocent passengers on board.

Go look at what's getting reported and then tell me I'm wrong. Most of these bad apples scenarios arise from a use-of-force incident, right? It's because a police officer used excessive force— at least in the eyes of the public. "How could this senseless loss of life have been prevented? How can we stop the police from murdering our loved ones?"

My response is that if people didn't resist arrest or fight with the cops, there wouldn't be a need for use of force. Period. Even in the very, very small percentage of times that resistance does result in actual excessive force, it could have been avoided with simple compliance. We're not coming in guns-a-blazin' unless the perpetrator has already escalated the situation to that point. Stop resisting arrest. Stop trying to get away. Stop throwing your body around while screaming, "I am complying!" Stop lunging for our weapons, and stop kicking, biting, and spitting on us. It's the equivalent of an airline passenger throwing themselves around the cockpit mid-flight, flipping switches and pushing buttons that are going to result in harm to other people. Of course you're going to experience a show of force, because there are hundreds of other lives in the immediate vicinity that you're putting in danger. Sit in your fucking seat and eat your peanuts.

I keep bringing this number up, and I'm going to continue doing so, because I want it to stay in your mind: there are nearly 800,000 police officers in the United States, and they made or received just under 260,000,000 contacts with the general public in 2018. Of those contacts, 0.3% involved pointing or shooting a gun, irrespective of ethnicity. Just how much of an apple is 0.3%?[4]

Airline pilots certainly undergo a lot of training, but does any of that training involve handling an aggressor with a deadly weapon? They might mention it in the safety manual, I suppose. I imagine it's quite stressful to fly a plane safely and be responsible for all those lives as it is, but what happens if somebody rushes the cabin or stabs an attendant? Well, firstly, you're probably watching a Harrison Ford film. Secondly, that kind of thing just normally doesn't happen outside Hollywood. The level of stress between a typical airline pilot and a typical beat cop is not in the same ballpark. And the higher the stress level, the higher the chance of mistakes. Rock is comparing bad apples to oranges and, while funny, it doesn't align. Worse, it's perpetuating the stigma that these fine men and women are somehow inept at their jobs, which couldn't be further from the truth. If you're going to draw ridiculous comparisons, at least get your facts straight.

There's no other profession like police work (other than military service). There's no way that members of the public can really understand police work without having done the job themselves. When people don't understand something, they often make assumptions or even fabricate myths like the ones I've discussed above. They're missing the mark. People with good old-fashioned common sense acknowledge that not everyone understands what law enforcement entails, and the best thing to do is stand back and let the professionals handle it.

CHAPTER SIX
MAY I ARREST YOU?

Let me run you through a traffic stop in 2021.

Let's say I'm out on what's called a "drug interdiction"—which just means I'm there to interrupt the exchange or trade of drugs—and I see a car full of people leave what I suspect to be a drug house. I'm very interested in this car because I suspect that the driver is transporting drugs, but I can't pull him over for just this suspicion. But maybe he's nervous and he starts speeding, or weaving, or runs through a stop sign (or makes four left turns). So I pull him over and approach the vehicle.

"Hi there. I'm Officer Silvester. I stopped you because you were going a little fast through that twenty-five zone. Do you have your information? License, registration, proof of insurance? Thanks so much. Hey, is there anything illegal in the car? Do you have any drugs? Weapons, or anything like that?"

If I believe that these people are hiding something or that there might indeed be drugs inside the car, I'll call for a canine unit to come and run his dog. I radio it in and, out of necessity, make the car wait until he arrives from whatever call he was on prior. Most departments don't have more than a couple of canine units, because they're highly specialized and quite expensive, so there's no guarantee that they can arrive within a moment's notice. Sometimes it takes a while.

Now, normally, what I would do is stand there and watch out for the canine officer to provide cover or backup in case something comes up. His attention is on controlling his dog, so he can't focus on the people that are in the car or the myriad threats that might emerge there. As you can imagine, it takes a considerable amount of concentration to do his job, so trying to keep one eye on his dog and one eye on the vehicle occupants makes him blind to both.

However, with recent case law and top-down interference, I (as the initiating officer of the traffic stop) can no longer stand there and protect this canine unit with my support. The reason?

It prolongs the traffic stop outside the scope of the original violation.

As in, I, watching out for the well-being of a fellow officer with my vigilance and training so that he can give full attention to fulfilling his specialized duties, am adding precious seconds to the duration of the traffic stop—which courts have interpreted as a violation of the driver's Fourth Amendment rights.

If I call for a canine unit, he has to show up immediately or not at all, and I have to already be in the process of writing the citation when he gets there. The instant the citation is written, I have to give it to the driver and get him on his way, because the clock is ticking. The US Supreme Court ruled in *Illinois v. Caballes* that the procedure of a canine unit performing its duty is acceptable, provided the search is not "unreasonably" long. If I prolong that stop a second longer than is absolutely necessary to deal with the primary violation, absent any reasonable suspicion that a secondary violation or crime has occurred and warrants further investigation (and the decision for that all comes down to the ruling of the judge), then *I'm* in violation of the driver's Fourth Amendment rights.

In case you're interested, I just so happen to have the full Fourth Amendment right here for your perusal. There's not much to it, truth be told:

"The right of the people to be secure in their persons, houses, papers, and effects, against unreasonable searches and seizures, shall not be violated, and no warrants shall issue, but upon probable cause, supported by oath or affirmation, and particularly describing the place to be searched, and the persons or things to be seized."

Maybe you have a law degree, maybe you don't, but does it say anything right there about a countdown clock for justice? Maybe I need my eyes checked, but I don't see it. I get that I shouldn't jam up someone's day at a routine stop, but if there's reasonable suspicion of crime, it takes however long it takes.

The idea that I'm inconveniencing the daily routines of this driver with added time is ludicrous. Most stops are over within a few minutes. But, as it turns out, the more laws you break, the longer the stop takes.

Cops are not there for the public's convenience. We don't wave you down at your earliest leisure and ask politely, "Hey, when you get a sec, may I arrest you?" The point is, an officer's job is made more difficult because of obstacles thrown at him from every direction. The criminals, the administrators, the media, the citizens—even the courts are putting up roadblocks left and right.

When is the last time you remember waiting in the drive-thru at McDonald's? I don't mean when they're between fry batches and they ask you to pull into one of those side parking spots. I mean when is the last time you actually waited in the line of cars for food?

I remember waiting for such a long time when I was younger, but that's all changed now. They've streamlined the process.

Now, you pull up to the little ordering panel and ask for all the chicken nuggets they possess. And a Diet Coke. And you immediately pull ahead to pay, which takes the briefest of moments, and then you roll up to the food window, where you're immediately handed a huge bag of all the chicken nuggets they possess, and a Diet Coke. It takes longer to get the paper wrapper off the straw than it did for you to place, pay for, and receive your entire order. How do they do it so quickly?

One reason is COVID. The dining rooms all shut down, so the drive-thrus became the only way to get fast food (on a side note, if you were a food-runner during the pandemic, thank you). Another reason is they narrowed their menu down. You don't have as many options at McDonald's as you did a year or two ago, including no all-day breakfast. But, you get your pre-made food faster. The McD's bigwigs want to shave seconds off of each order, and they want you to know about it. Some locations have those readout screens with the total number of seconds it's taking the workers inside to wrap up your Big Mac and throw it out the window at you. It depends on what all you order but, most of the time, it's under two minutes. I've had some orders that went through in thirty seconds.

What if it's longer, though? What if it takes them a few more seconds than you're anticipating? Doesn't matter the reason; could be a malfunctioning fountain drink hose, could be a misprinted wrapper, could be that someone had your order in-hand and slipped, so they had to start all over again. You don't see any of that from your car. All you know is that the guy in front of you got out of there faster than you, and the lady behind you looks impatient, and now you've missed the green light on the way out. And you're still hungry.

A normal person would just wait. You're the one who decided to stop at McDonald's, you're the one who just had to have a McRib at 3:45, so you have to be prepared to endure the process to get what you want. But there are loads of videos of people having a public freak-out about not getting their drive-thru order "in time." Seriously, if you want to see people throwing absolute fits over nothing, look them up. They toss food on workers, spit in the window, slam into the building with their cars, and the list just goes on and on. It really puts things in perspective, at least for me. It's also good training for us, because the police spend way too much time contacting morons like this. Again, we like camera footage.

This entitled mentality is toxic, and it breeds intolerance, and it breeds unfair expectations. It gives rise to rules and restrictions that actually impede the law and endanger people. Where is this all heading? What impact will this dumbfuckery lead to in the very near future? Let's go back to that traffic stop and try it their way.

I'm sitting in my booth by a four-way intersection. The sign on the booth says, "Welcome" with no indication of its purpose. I'm not a cop anymore, I'm a "Reporting Helper." Instead of a badge, I have a laminated sheet of paper that hangs around my neck containing all of my personal information, including my full name, my home address, my social, my personal cell number, the names and birth dates of all my family members, along with their home addresses, a list of phrases and names for quick reference that people can use to insult me, and an 800 number that links directly to the attorney who expedites lawsuits for anyone who feels like suing me that day. I get fifteen calls a day, even though I almost never interact with anyone in person.

We had to get rid of our guns because they were too intimidating. We traded out our tasers and batons for Wiffle bats and kazoos, which were at least something, but then someone got a rash from a plastic allergy and that was that. Now I just have my hands, which I can't use because I don't have clearance. I guess I have my voice, but I have to be very careful how and when I use it, because I'm not supposed to give any indication of authority or use a tone of accusation.

No, I'm just sitting in my booth in case anyone wants to report themselves for a crime. I don't get much traffic these days, but that's only because the system's working and no one commits crimes to report anymore. I heard we're just waiting on one more bill to pass that does away with Reporting Helpers altogether. What a time to be alive. The eradication of crime.

But wait, what's this? Through the bars on my booth, I see a car approach. The driver pulls right up to the window. I take care not to look in the vehicle in case there are innocent bystanders inside; I'm not allowed to presume that everyone who comes to my booth actually wants help reporting their own crime. They could just be there to collect my information and move on. I wait to speak until spoken to.

"We don't have any drugs," says the driver, holding drugs. They must not be his, I remind myself. Thank God for my acceptance-conditioning training.

"How may I help you today?" I ask in my cheeriest tone.

"Fuck you and quit disrespecting me." He snorts a line of coke off his steering wheel and passes the baggie to the other passengers. Wait, no, it only *appears* to be coke. I recall my supervisor saying that people snort white powders for all manner of very personal, private, and medical reasons, and there's no way to confirm that this substance is indeed a drug product. Huge relief.

"I am so sorry, sir." I begin my court-ordered Recitation of Forgiveness, making sure to dip my head lower than the car door handles with the customary bowing. "Forgive me, forgive me, forgive me. I am nothing and shall remain nothing. Forgive me," repeated seven times.

"I want to report a crime," he says. I reach for my official Reporting Helper form, but it's difficult because I'm handcuffed to my chair.

"Absolutely, sir. May I please get your name?"

"It's not for me. I want to report you."

"Sir, that's very understandable. What can I get started for you?" I grab a different form with my name already printed at the top under "Perpetrator." I keep stacks of these on hand.

"For one thing, disrespect."

"Got it, sir, thank you. One charge of disrespect."

"And you're racist."

"Racism charge, got it. Do you want that with or without evidence?"

"Without."

"Great choice. May I interest you in a secondary offense? Simple assault or criminal misconduct?"

"Nah. Let's do unwarranted surveillance. Oh, and witness tampering."

"Done and done, sir. Will that be all today?"

"Nope. You're over your time now."

"Of course, my mistake. Adding 'unlawful detainment' to the order."

"That's all for now."

"Okay, thank you for using Reporting Helpers. It's been a pleasure to serve you."

This is a fucking ridiculous example, isn't it? Doesn't it paint the wrong picture and exaggerate all the issues? I must be way off-base with this kind of thinking, because the USA is a land of freedom and greatness and there's no way we'd sit back and just allow this kind of shit to happen.

Except we do. We do it when we vote, or worse, refuse to vote. When we sit back and let these voices dictate how our country should be run, silencing our police officers and pushing them down into a corner where they're afraid to open their mouths because they have bills to pay and families to care for. Since when did upholding the law become an infringement of human rights? Don't human rights exist (and continue to exist) *because* of the law? Well, for good or for bad, not everyone interprets the law the same way.

The current trend is restricting police officers from performing their assigned duties. I think I've sufficiently laid out just how difficult the job already is, but there's a large movement to hamstring the already-limited police force and, if it's not stopped, we can be sure that our country will look like a scene out of *Escape from New York*.

Take their guns. Take their restraint holds. Take their tasers. Take their badges. Take their power. Take their rights.

So let's look at that, shall we? Without guns, there's no meeting force with greater force. Anyone with a gun on the streets now rules without question. They can shoot whoever they like, and the only fear of repercussion is if another armed citizen happens to feel like shooting them.

If the trend continues, there will be no police. Droves of confused individuals think that's a good thing. A cheer goes up whenever the topic arises. No cops, no worries, right?

There's a common saying in the police world: cops deal with 6% of the population 94% of the time, and 94% of the population 6% of the time. It's that 6% that makes police officers necessary. Most people will go their entire lives without any impactful interactions with the police, other than maybe a traffic stop or two. So it's easy for some people to be convinced that they don't need the cops. "We get along just fine without them," say people who don't understand crime. They're not leading crime-free lives because people are inherently good and just not committing crimes against each other; people treat each other like garbage. The reason they're able to go about their day without being overwhelmed by criminals is because the police stop them. That's it. That's the secret. The cops bust lawbreakers and remove them from society, so society can function. If some dude waves a gun in front of a school bus, we take him away. No more threat.

But raise enough complaints against the cops and someone's going to take notice. That garbage treatment of each other seems hotly directed at police officers most of the time. "Officer Silvester was rude to me!" I don't want to belabor the point, but one call, one complaint, can end my career. This mentality comes from the same line of thinking that the people throwing food at the drive-thru cashier have.

"I've been wronged and demand compensation for being offended. Since I can't get financial compensation, I'll settle for someone getting fired."

So, well done, you got that food service worker fired. They were probably in high school, trying to earn some gas money, and never did anything wrong in the first place, but now they're gone.

Your anger is sated for now, but they have a permanent record of termination from possibly the only job they've had to that point. What's their outlook on trying for Job Number Two when it shows they were fired for a customer complaint? It's not good.

But that young person is out, what, two shifts worth of training and the cost of their work ID? No offense to them, because paychecks matter, but that's a drop in the bucket for an officer of the law.

Eligibility to be a cop depends on several factors. You have to be at least twenty-one years old, have a high school diploma, GED, or equivalent, and you have to pass a physical test. From there, you move on to an interview process, which can last hours. There's usually a panel of four or five people, at least in my experience, and it can be very intimidating for young officers. If you pass the interview portion, you have to undergo a psychological evaluation, which is pretty grueling. Mine involved three hundred rather invasive questions in a questionnaire format. After that, you take a written test (surprise, critical thinking and communication skills are a must for cops). Then you undergo a polygraph test. If you've never had the misfortune of taking a polygraph, they're uncomfortable at best. I don't care how clean your piss is or how unsullied your past; they're made to get you to second-guess yourself. You start thinking to yourself, "Did I jam a flat-screen up my ass and accidentally steal it that one time at Walmart?"

Assuming you've made it this far, the next step is an extensive (and they mean it) background check. They check your previous employment, your criminal history, call your mom, your neighbors, your extended family members. They ask around about you. They go through your social media and all that that entails. Sometimes they run a credit check just to see how likely you are to be taken advantage of, or if you have uncontrolled habits. If everything looks good, you move ahead.

Now you're employed, but you're not ready yet. You go to the academy, and that's another fifteen weeks at the very least, depending on what state you work in. Some academies are thirty-four-week programs. To put some perspective on that, full-term pregnancy is forty weeks. The academy is its own beast. You're up at 5:45 every morning for PT. After training, which usually consisted of a two-mile run, some sprints, perhaps laps in the pool, you grab a quick breakfast and then it's eight straight hours of classroom instruction: roleplaying scenarios for domestic violence and de-escalation techniques, firearms training, driving instruction for stuff like PIT (Pursuit Intervention Technique) maneuvers, TVI (Tactical Vehicle Intervention), and EVOC (Emergency Vehicle Operator Course), radio operations, traffic stops, patrol procedures, interrogation techniques, first aid, arrest techniques, fingerprinting, report-writing skills, death notifications, crash reconstruction etc., etc., etc. Then it's dinner and possibly more classroom time until 9 or 10 at night; then it's lights out. Some academies might end the day with a five-mile run for good measure.

And you do that over and over and over until it's done. They regularly test you throughout the academy training, and many of the tests are extensive and grueling because they have to know you're getting the material. It's intense, and not just anybody can handle it.

And yes, we learn state law at the same time. The Idaho code book, with all its statutes, is a good four or five inches thick, and we have to go through almost the entire thing. I say almost because we're not expected to learn every single item—mainly the criminal and traffic codes—unlike an attorney with eight or ten years of schooling. Still, it's a whole lot, and it's not a stretch to say that, when it comes to certain laws, common police officers are expected to meet or exceed the level of an attorney's knowledge in a given situation and be able to act on that at a moment's notice. When strenuous moments arise, we don't have three weeks to prepare documents, arguments, and counterpoints. We have to act the instant it's called for, and those actions have to be impeccable the first time, every time.

Imagine being an officer effecting a traffic stop. You have to watch the occupants of the vehicle the whole time to ensure they're not a threat, because they could be; anyone could be in that vehicle. You also have to be aware of traffic around you. You don't want to exit your patrol car to be greeted by the grill of a semi truck barreling down the road. So you take your eyes off the driver to check for approaching vehicles, but not for too long, because the driver still might be a threat. You approach the vehicle cautiously, but with a smile. Remember, if the driver doesn't like the cut of your jib they can call your chief and complain. By the time you got back to the station, you'd already be under internal investigation for "conduct unbecoming" or some bullshit. So, you smile, while being hyper-vigilant and having a plan to kill them in case they become a deadly threat (I'm not joking in the least here). You also have to watch out for any approaching pedestrians or cars that pull up on your stop, which happens more than it should. Maybe the driver called a friend while you were stopping him and they're there to back him up. What if there are other passengers in the car? Now you have to worry about them as well. So, your attention is now divided amongst the driver, multiple passengers, however many pedestrians are walking by, passing motorists, and, if you've stopped in front of a residence, you have to check the windows to see if anyone is watching your traffic stop from inside the house, maybe pointing a rifle at you. Don't sit there and tell yourself this doesn't happen.

Is this stressing anyone else out? Because it should. It should make people sit back and go, "Wow, I had no idea what they go through. Here I am casting aspersions on these incredible men and women, and now I'm not even sure I'd have what it takes to be them."

I'm not trying to pick a fight, but how much training did you need for your current job? Was it more than nine hundred hours? Have you spent nine hundred hours doing anything besides sleeping or watching TikToks? I'm not calling you lazy; I want you to think about it. This isn't some slightly demanding job; this is a complete overhaul of yourself as a person, and you will emerge as something new on the other side.

If and when you graduate from the academy, you go to your department and training continues for another three to four months beyond that. You do your four-phase field training at that time and, if you're approved, you get your ride-alone status. Beyond this, you're required to maintain at least forty hours of training per year in order to retain your certification as a police officer. That barely scratches the surface of how many hundreds of hours most cops reel in. We're constantly undergoing more training and more education, and there's really no end to how much we need. There's always something else to learn. Officers must stay abreast of the latest trends in technology being used to share and conceal child pornography, and what methods drug traffickers are using to mule their product into your city. We have to stay up to date with the travel patterns of biker gangs and the strategies they employ to isolate officers on the road and attack them.

Let's say I've been on the job for years. I started with my basic certificate when I graduated from the academy, and then I advanced to an intermediate certificate, then an advanced certificate by committing myself to becoming a better cop. By the time I retire, I will have thousands of training hours and anywhere between twenty and thirty years on the job. That's an awesome trove of invaluable experience.

But my chances of making it that far, at least in light of recent events, are almost nil. In the eyes of the public, the police are now the enemy. Some people seem to think we're either drafted out of prison or plucked off the street, handed a gun with unlimited ammo, and told to go drive around and harass citizens for laughs. Here's the law book if you get a chance or feel like taking a look between reloads. Otherwise, just go ham.

We aren't fast-food workers. We didn't just show up this morning when they were handing out badges and say, "What the hell, I'll be a cop for a while." This is our livelihood. Not only that—for most of us, it's our passion. We can't see ourselves doing anything other than just being cops, because the glove fits so well and, chances are, it doesn't fit anywhere else. It's not just that one complaint call can somehow end a career (but believe me, that sucks enough); it's that the fallout from that ended career carries so much additional baggage. You lose your job, yes, but also your pension. Your benefits. Your health coverage. Your retirement fund. The only chance you have at a rehire is likely moving out of state, and even then, it's slim to none. One round of bills without insurance is enough to cause irreparable damage to any savings account, not to mention the hit on your credit. You lose your self-respect and you sit back and say to yourself, "I thought I was trying to do some good in the world, but it bit me in the ass. Now what?"

I'd challenge all of these "defunders" to go spend one week auditing a police academy and see just how rigorous it is. Go see all the outrageous lengths cops go to to keep people safe from themselves. They'd see only a fraction of what we go through, but it might be enough to shed that mentality that drives them to hate us so badly. It might have an impact on steering away from crippling law enforcement to the point they're unable to act for fear of overblown retaliation.

If the narrative doesn't change, extremist legislation or not, we're going to run out of cops. The rate at which police officers are being killed, being fired for bullshit reasons, or walking off the job because they don't want to deal with the first two things, is increasing by the minute. Where will we be in five years? They won't need to defund the police, because society is doing it for them. We have outraged voices over the death of career criminals, but not a damn word about all the undeniable good that cops are responsible for every day. No one seems to give a shit. It's like the US is sitting there with a whack-a-mole hammer over the head of each police officer, and it can't stand.

In certain areas in the Middle East, if two people are involved in a car crash, it's their responsibility to figure out who's at fault. Someone has to go to jail, because a law was broken, so they yell and scream and fight to blame each other. You might have seen videos of two guys absolutely losing their minds over a fender bender, but that's how their system works. It's a defense mechanism, and they have to reach an agreement before the authorities arrive (clock's ticking!). Otherwise, they both go to jail.

This is just one small example of what happens when people are left to police themselves. Imagine heading to the grocery store and someone crashing into your car, so you have to outshout them and somehow find a way to make them admit guilt; otherwise, you're behind bars instead of enjoying your homemade spaghetti. If only you'd had a highly qualified, highly trained, incredibly helpful law enforcement professional on hand to walk you through the process. It's a shame the country decided they were better off without those worthless cops.

But, with the cops gone, who's handling the murderers? The rapists? The pedophiles, the arsonists, the burglars? That guy who waved a gun at that school bus full of kids? Enlighten me: what's your *cul-de-sac* posse going to do about him? Because when "talking him down" fails and he starts drawing a bead on kids, I'll bet your plan shifts to some excessive force pretty goddamn fast. You might even resort to a chokehold if need be. Without police, these criminals would run rampant through the streets, endangering everyone. There's no question about it.

Whenever there's a big push for policy change, like the abolition of law enforcement, who stands to benefit from that? When it comes down to it, you know who doesn't want cops around? Criminals. Those who want to willfully break the law without repercussion.

Think about that next time you're rolling your eyes at those extra minutes on the clock while a cop tries his damnedest to do a thorough job of keeping your city safe. Even though you're being stopped for a minor moving violation, that officer is performing a duty that you, as the taxpayer, have commissioned him to do. Cops don't need permission to eradicate crime; that's what the badge is for, and you bet your ass the officer behind that badge paid his dues. That thing was earned.

Nobody likes the referee, but he ensures the game is played in a fair and orderly fashion. Police officers do their job with reasonable objectivity, which might be labeled as discriminatory or unfair by some, but having an emotional reaction doesn't mean there's been an injustice. Stop complaining about the rules of the game and let the ref do his job.

Pretty please.

CHAPTER SEVEN
FREE TO DOX

At around 4:32 p.m. on April 20, 2021, a call came in to the Columbus, Ohio dispatch from the 3000 block of Legion Lane. The caller, clearly in distress, shouted, "We got [inaudible] trying to fight us! Trying to stab us! Put their hands on our grandma! Get here now!" Screams rang out in the background.

At 4:44 p.m., first responder Officer Nicholas Reardon and two other officers arrive at the scene, which is already chaotic and violent. Officer Reardon exits his cruiser and asks, "What's going on? What's going on?" and receives no response from anyone. Instead, an unidentified male (allegedly a parent or guardian in the foster care system) throws a girl to the ground in front of Reardon and proceeds to kick her in the head. To the male's right, 16-year-old Ma'Khia Bryant can be seen with a knife in her hand. Amid the ensuing melee of shoving, kicking, and hitting from the gathered group, Bryant, brandishing a knife, charges and pins an unidentified female dressed in pink clothing against a car. Bryant's intent to kill is clear as she maneuvers the knife over and under the girl's arms, weaving around her desperate defenses for a direct stab. Bryant screams, "I'm gonna stab the fuck out of you, bitch!" Reardon warns, "Hey, hey, hey. Get down! Get down! Get down!" while Bryant tenses her muscles and positions her knife to fatally stab the other girl. Reardon, recognizing deadly force, draws his firearm and fires four instantaneous shots into Bryant's center mass, and she slumps against the very car door she had used to pin the other girl. This all happens within ten seconds of the officers' arrival. Reardon keeps his weapon drawn—but down—in case further threats manifest and, once it appears the other citizens are momentarily at bay, moves to assist in relocating Bryant for CPR measures. The attempted murder weapon, the knife, lies to Bryant's left side, just out of her grasp.

Officer Nicholas Reardon not only saved the life of the young girl in pink, he did so without endangering the lives of any others who were present, and he did it with a split-second decision that correctly identified and eliminated the lethal threat. Go watch the footage, then watch it again. He didn't shoot the man kicking the girl in the head right in front of him. He didn't fire downrange into a crowd or nearby residences. He didn't try to aim for Bryant's hand holding the knife, which would have pierced her arm and struck the other girl. He didn't shoot Bryant's foot or leg, permitting her to continue the attack. He didn't open fire on the group. Experts going through the body cam footage in slow motion, frame by frame, struggle to keep up with just how perfectly Reardon performed in that one brief instant of law enforcement.

Did Ma'Khia Bryant, a minor who was allegedly an honor student, "a beautiful, sweet girl," who was just a teenager, have to die?

Yes.

Let me be absolutely clear. Bryant didn't die because she was a minor. She didn't die because she was an honor student. She didn't die because she was in foster care. She didn't die because she was Black. She didn't die because cops are racist. She didn't die because cops are trigger-happy. She didn't die because of her socioeconomic status.

She died because she attempted to murder another human being with a knife.

Nothing she did before that moment matters. Nothing. The only thing that matters is that, in that moment, for whatever reason, she chose to kill. She died because her attempt at murder was stopped by a cop.

No matter how I put this, there are still going to be people who have a knee-jerk reaction, mistake my words, and claim I'm saying that her life doesn't matter. Life is precious, but did that cross *her* mind when she picked up a deadly weapon? She was a young girl who deserved every good thing the world could offer her, but she lost all rights to any future the moment she tried to drive that knife blade into the body of another person. The situation surpassed the point of de-escalation techniques; it surpassed the point of tasers or pepper spray or restraints; the only recourse to save a life was deadly force *because Ma'Khia Bryant chose that outcome with her actions*.

It is a tragedy of immense magnitude for anyone who hears the story, but then the story gets twisted to further various agendas. The media have gone to great lengths to portray this event as a miscarriage of justice, an easily preventable disaster, and a failure of law enforcement as a whole. It's somehow been cast as the fault of Officer Reardon, and the fault of the other officers who were present, the fault of the Columbus PD, the fault of police officers as a whole, the fault of systemic racism, the fault of white people everywhere. They've taken quotes from Bryant's family, her extended family, her loved ones, her friends, the neighbors, the bystanders, the passersby. We've heard from city officials, state officials, special interest groups, and on and on, but you know who we haven't heard from? Who we won't hear from?

Nicholas Reardon.

He's not supposed to count. The media doesn't want his input, his opinion, or his reaction to being called out that day to make an impossible choice of taking a life to save a life, a decision that will impact him for the rest of his days. No human should have to make that choice, but it was forced on him by a murderous street fight. Forget all the good he's done (including this instance). Forget all the crimes he's stopped, the people he's protected, his service to the country as a US Air National Guardsman.

In the eyes of millions, he's nothing more than a child killer.

A large portion of these millions have been spoon-fed this opinion by celebrities misusing their status and influence to spread lies. One such is "KingJames" himself. Hours after the shooting, before any department investigation report or press release of information, LeBron James—winner of four NBA championships, four NBA MVP Awards, four Finals MVP Awards, and two Olympic gold medals—shared a picture of Officer Reardon to his Twitter account with the tagline, "YOU'RE NEXT #ACCOUNTABILITY".

At the time of the tweet (April 21st, 2021), James had 49.7 million followers.

Understand, this man has a net worth of over $500 million. He pulls in about $44 million a year from his basketball salary, and another $55 million in products he endorses. He has a $32 million shoe contract with Nike. He endorses Coca-Cola, AT&T, GMC, Beats Electronics, Blaze Pizza, 2K Sports, even a goddamn luggage company.

He is paid millions and millions and millions of dollars to

LeBron James ✓
@KingJames

YOU'RE NEXT ⧖
#ACCOUNTABILITY

support various products or concepts because his doing so leads to increased sales for these companies. That means every time he picks up a Coke, countless droves of people run out and buy Coke. Every time a basketball camera catches a glimpse of his Nikes, millions rush to secure their Nike purchases.

And every time he posts stupid shit like this hit piece on social media, millions jump to the same cop-hating false conclusions that he does. There are a total of twenty-four countries and independent territories in the world with smaller populations than his Twitter account.[5]

His tweets reach more people than BBC Breaking News, NASA, Oprah Winfrey, Sports Center, and ESPN. You read that right: he impacts more people than sports itself.[6]

Imagine having this level of clout and saying, "I want you, my nation of loyal followers, to go find Officer Nicholas Reardon, who is a child killer according to the laws I interpret as a basketball star, in Columbus, Ohio, and shoot him dead in the street," and getting away with it. Scot-free.

This is called doxing, which you may not have heard of before. It comes from the same word as "doc" or "document," and it means to post personal information in a public space about another individual or group, typically with malicious intent. The definition is behind the times, however, as the current connotation revolves around a publicized call-to-arms for vigilante justice.

And when doxing applies specifically to cops, it carries the threat of death.

In the wake of the LeBron tweet, our nation saw an influx of officer deaths as the result of ambushes or other outright physical attacks. One in particular was a corporal with the Delmar Police Department in Delaware.

Keith Heacook was called to a disturbance. The suspect, Randon Wilkerson, had attacked his roommate and then an elderly couple. When the corporal arrived on scene, Wilkerson, lying in wait, attacked him. Heacook was knocked unconscious and, as he lay on the pavement, Wilkerson stomped on his head repeatedly with his boot. This tragedy was but one of the officer murders that we saw in the aftermath of the Ma'Khia Bryant incident. Even though people like Wilkerson aren't directly connected to LeBron James, James, along with other "woke" celebrities who use their tremendous influence to incentivize violence against police officers, should share some culpability in these officers' deaths.

James' tweet, in no uncertain terms, called for the death of Officer Nicholas Reardon. An eye for an eye, a death for a death. We have yet to see if any of those nearly 50 million followers will try to take King James' dictum to kill but, even if someone did, the current laws do not hold LeBron James accountable for putting out a hit on a certified officer in good standing through the use of his substantial social platform. Aside from a possible loss of public opinion, he incurs no legal penalty, fine, or jail time. And in the meantime, he just gets more press.

Shortly after the "YOU'RE NEXT" tweet, the official Twitter account for the National Fraternal Order of Police (FOP) issued the following statement (@GLFOP, April 21st, 2021):

After this and further backlash about the tweet, and probably under heavy legal advisement, James took it down, but the damage was already done. His endorsement of hatred and violence against cops had already reached a huge number of people. He later tweeted a non-apology that pointed the finger at everyone else with the following:

Since we're on the topic, what's LeBron's accountability here? Obviously, the NBA isn't going to suspend, fine, or sanction their all-star cash cow, and they still haven't. He could have posted a genuine apology. He could have said, "I apologize to the officer and his family for putting them at risk, and I apologize to the rest of the country for further tearing it apart after we have already been divided. I also apologize to the NBA for misrepresenting them and bringing them to disrepute." But he didn't, and he won't. Every time a critical event occurs involving cops, he weighs in on it as if he has any functional knowledge of these situations or the police work behind them. At the very least, it's irresponsible. On the other hand, the realistic one, he's championing for death and violence.

Where is our legislation for this? Where are the higher-ups breathing down his neck? We have so many enraged people out in the streets chanting for the deaths of officers. I don't see anyone outside of the LA Lakers' arena breaking windows and calling for LeBron's suspension. Do you? Am I missing something?

Maybe the truth of the matter is that some people like having their hatred directed, and cops are easy targets.

Imagine the tables were flipped. Imagine a cop with 50 million followers comes out and says, "I want one of you to go kill LeBron James." Can you envision the shitstorm that would erupt? That cop would instantaneously be fired, fined, and jailed. There'd be no question. But that wouldn't be enough. The nation would lash out, demanding further recompense for the outrageous statement against their beloved basketball player. The special interest groups would lobby for police reform, and insist on a full-scale investigation into police departments across the country to root out the cause of this insidious, systemic corruption.

Well, they've already done all that.

In June of 2019, two attorneys calling themselves the Plain View Project (PVP), founded by Emily Baker-White and a hired paralegal, compiled a database of Facebook posts from local police officers of the Philadelphia Police Department that they deemed to "endorse violence, racism, and bigotry".[7] The PVP "researchers" took screenshots of any post, comment, video, or status from anyone they determined to be connected to the police department, totaling about 300 individuals and spanning years of Facebook usage. PVP redacted the names and/or faces of any non-officers in the database, but made sure to include the names and faces of everyone they assumed were cops.

According to the Police Advisory Committee's (PAC) 2020 report, "The most common themes present in the officers' Facebook content were Islamophobia (358 instances), making light of use of force (284 instances), mocking opposing viewpoints (253 instances), and coded racist language (231 instances)."

And then PVP posted everything to the public, along with metadata that used publicly available information to match the posts to the officer's badge numbers, titles, and salaries.

Before the Philadelphia PD could process any measure of response, the social backlash had already exploded across all media platforms. Baker-White, with some work as a student attorney under her belt and a BA in Politics, had lit the fuse. Citizens were outraged and in rolled the calls for the defunding of the police department, the termination/resignation of every police officer, and even the deaths of certain officers. Protests and community meetings took place one after the other, all fueled by rage against the police. While that Dumpster fire roared and Baker-White sat back to watch her website hits go through the roof, the PPD reached out to PAC and the help of local attorney firm, Ballard Spahr, to review the database and try to reach some direction on how to salvage the fallout.

The PAC and Ballard Spahr opted to measure each Facebook post exactly how PVP had done it: investigate any post or comment that they determined could, in their opinion, undermine the public's trust.

Sound a little subjective to you? Not yet? Let's continue.

Per the PAC and Ballard Spahr recommendations (i.e. dictates), the PPD proceeded to discipline its officers, which included terminations, suspensions, sanctions, forced retirements, forced counseling, and on and on. Careers ended, pensions, salaries, and benefits discontinued, and charges against the police officers in question piled higher and deeper by the minute. In total, 338 internal investigations were launched, a handful of which are still ongoing today. If you can recall how stringent the supervisors were who conducted my own internal investigation, you might have some idea of how overwhelmingly intense these proceedings must have been.

Now, officers cannot be punished just for posting content someone *might* consider offensive. Even if the posts were offensive, they're still constitutionally protected as free speech. In order to legally take disciplinary action against an officer, the PPD had to be able to prove a few things.

Way back in 1968, a teacher named Marvin Pickering wrote a letter to a local newspaper in which he criticized his own school board for misuse of public funds. According to Pickering, the school used money to sod their football field instead of paying their teachers' salaries, and he pointed it out to the media. He got fired, took it to a local court and got overruled, then took it to the

Supreme Court, where he won 8-1. This case set the precedent for all First Amendment cases involving public employees.

From that point on, any question of a public employee's freedom of speech must pass what's now called the Pickering Connick Test (or Pickering Balancing Test). The test hinges on an initial threshold question: "Did the employee speak on matters of public concern?"

"If a public employee was disciplined for expression that is characterized as more of a private grievance, then the employer prevails. If, however, a public employee spoke on a matter of public concern, then the court proceeds to the second part of the test often called the balancing prong".[8]

If it's determined that the employee spoke on matters of public concern, the balancing test asks these three questions:

1. Is the employer's prediction of the disruption that such speech will cause reasonable?

2. Does the potential for disruption of the workplace outweigh the value of the speech?

3. Did the employer take an adverse employment action not in retaliation for the employee's speech, but because of the potential for disruption?

Subjective, subjective, subjective. When the best our courts can do is this vague language ("prediction," "potential," "not in retaliation"), we're opening ourselves up to bias and misjudgment, and it infringes on our First Amendment rights. In the case of police officers, the effect is immediate.

Pickering held sway until 2006, when a 5-4 majority ruling, led by Justice Anthony M. Kennedy in *Garcetti v. Ceballos*, determined that "when public employees make statements pursuant to their official duties, the employees are not speaking as citizens for First

Amendment purposes, and the Constitution does not insulate their communications from employer discipline."

I know I'm dumping a lot of information down your throat, but did you see where, again, public workers (including and perhaps especially police officers) *lose their constitutional rights*? A 5-4 ruling isn't exactly evidence that people saw eye to eye on this matter. In fact, some of the other justices spoke out against the ruling.

"Justices John Paul Stevens, David H. Souter, and Stephen G. Breyer each wrote dissenting opinions. Stevens criticized the majority's decision as 'misguided' and stated that 'the notion that there is a categorical difference between speaking as a citizen and speaking in the course of one's employment is quite wrong,'"[9]

So the PPD, along with Ballard Spahr, had to sift through this highly publicized mess, with all its subjective, vague language, and come up with some kind of standard with which to gauge the offensiveness of these Facebook posts.

The 2020 PAC report on the PVP states that, "If Ballard Spahr determined that officers were speaking as citizens in their PVP Database content, they then had to determine if the officers were speaking about a matter of public concern. Matters of public concern are defined broadly, as anything that can 'be fairly considered as relating to any matter of political, social, or other concern to the community,' or when it 'is a subject of legitimate news interest; that is, a subject of general interest and of value and concern to the public'.[10] Courts look at the 'content, form, and context' of the speech[11], and also take into account the employee's motivation, 'as well as whether it is important to our system of self-government that the expression take place'."[12]

Find me one post on all of social media—take your pick of any platform—that meets these criteria. Find me one casserole recipe, or gym selfie, or brunch pic that's "of general interest and of value and concern to the public." You won't succeed. The public doesn't give a shit about your life hacks, or your makeup routine, or your kid's birthday party. They're too busy utilizing their First Amendment rights to post about their personal interests.

By their own admission on the website, PVP says, "To be clear, our concern is not whether these posts and comments are protected by the First Amendment... The posts and comments are open to various interpretations. We do not know what a poster meant when he or she typed them; we only know that when we saw them, they concerned us. We have shared these posts because we believe they should start a conversation..."[13]

The Plain View Project didn't start "a national dialogue about police." Emily Baker-White and her cohorts did nothing more than launch a defamatory torpedo at Philadelphia, then kick back and watch as the city tore itself apart.

And they've moved on to other departments as they pick up momentum and state funding. They're now backed by NACOLE (National Association for Civilian Oversight of Law Enforcement). Their database currently contains a growing collection of over 3,500 screenshots from police in eight different cities, including little ol' Twin Falls, Idaho.

According to PVP's sorry excuse for a disclaimer, "The posts and comments included in the database comprise portions of a user's public Facebook activity, and are therefore not intended to present a complete representation of each person's Facebook presence, or each person's views on any given subject."

Tell that to the people chanting for the deaths of these officers.

It's all part of the trend toward cancel culture. It's all ammunition in the war on cops. It's all just more doxing. And how many posts were made while the cops in question were on duty? What about off duty? Was there any attempt at distinction there, or was the assumption made that it didn't matter?

I want to specify some things before moving on. I've looked through the Facebook posts from the PVP database, and I want it known that many of the things said by these individuals are vile. There are clear-cut examples of debased minds at work, and the unfortunate truth of the matter is that some of them were shared by cops. There are posts involving blatant racism, mockery of rape and domestic violence, and encouragement of violence against perpetrators. These posts are despicable but, unreported by the media, there are far more categories for posts that are *not* malevolent.

Here are some further examples from the PAC's 2020 report: "Expressing opinion – A post or comment that states an opinion without including disparaging language or any other problematic content." PVP chose to flag posts that expressed opinion. Any time they came across an opinion from a police officer, regardless of intent or content, they added it to the database. In the case of D.F. Pace (a twenty-year veteran of the department), the opinion "Insightful point" earned him the reputation of bigotry by association. Pace has gone on to fight for his rights, so far with frustrating results, but I wish him the best of luck.

Another category was "Mocking opposing viewpoints – Posts and comments that disparage, villainize or explicitly mock political beliefs, police critics, and organizations such as Black Lives Matter, among other things, were included here." No one enjoys being mocked, but again, what's the distinction here? If someone posts "Defund the police!" and I reply, "Defund your face!" is that a disparaging remark against the post, or the poster? What about "I love Trump" versus "I hate Trump"? Did you read either response in a villainous tone, or was there some humor present? I can't say "subjective" enough, and I find it laughable that mocking opposing viewpoints is an egregious sin, but canceling someone out of existence for an opposing viewpoint is standard operating procedure for the woke.

"Coded racist language" was another category, which recognized that "Very few posts or comments [from Facebook] used racial slurs or overtly racist language." Instead, they reached for derogatory uses of words like "thug," "savage," or "animal." The report claimed 231 uses of this type of speech, none of which were actually racist. The best they could do is tack what they felt were negative terms onto an already overblown report to swell the results—in this case, determined by a blonde, white girl in her late twenties and her hirelings. She took the phrase, "Where there's smoke, there's fire" and flipped it to, "If there's no fire, start one and blame the cops."

"Dehumanizing language" came next: "Some examples include the use of offensive words such as 'retard,' 'cunt,' and 'toad.'" Again, not stellar language from the boys in blue, but being offensive doesn't remove their right to speak. You hear much worse from your friends on the weekend (if you don't, well, *good for you*). I sure do. "Also included were uses of language such as, 'scum,' 'scumbag,' 'POS' or 'piece of shit, [and] euphemisms such as 'productive member of society.'" What a joke. When a piece of shit murders his wife and child so he can go do crack with his girlfriend, he's a piece of shit. Call it what you will, but that's an impassioned reaction to a scumbag whose decisions have already dehumanized *himself*, and it doesn't change what's happened whether it's pointed out by a bus driver or a kindergartner or a cop.

The one that really gets under my skin is the category for "Shared post – no commentary – Any post or comment that is a neutral sharing of information via a link, article, video, etc." This means that any time a cop shared anything without saying a word about it, PVP grabbed the screenshot. No opinions given, no statements made, nothing more than clicking "Share" on something they came across. If it's "neutral sharing," then why the fuck is it on the list? I'll tell you why: it's to bolster the stats. "Shared post – no commentary" is the equivalent of nodding along during a dinner conversation and having someone nail you to the floor for endorsing the wrong opinion.

The last category I want to cover is really what brings this whole thing full circle. It's listed as "Vigilante justice – Any post or comment that encourages citizens to take the law into their own hands." This was part of the propulsion to internally investigate and subsequently suspend, fire, discipline, or otherwise punish the police officers of the Philadelphia Police Department. Examples include commending someone who beat up a rapist (great work, btw) and hoping for criminals to get beaten up in jail (some deserve exactly that).

You know what's another example of "vigilante justice" that needs to result in some punishment? How about a sports celebrity with 50 million followers who posts "YOU'RE NEXT" with the intent to bring harm to an upstanding officer of the law? It doesn't get much more "public" than LeBron James running his mouth to almost as many followers as *The New York Times* has. In fact, there are only twenty-five more followed Twitter accounts than LeBron's *on the planet*. Where is his state-funded, attorney-led oversight project to monitor, report, and enforce discipline any time he steps out of line (which is alarmingly often), not to mention when he sends out a call to end the life of another human being?

Where are the PVP groups to provide oversight for not just the NBA, but all sports? Where are they for celebrities? Or city officials? State officials? Politicians? Why are we allowing this war on police to continue? Does The Plain View Project provide oversight and transparency on behalf of its own members? What about larger umbrella organizations like NACOLE? Where are the links I can follow to see pointed, leading databases of their personal opinions and private interactions?

I reached out to ask these questions of the Philadelphia PAC, The Plain View Project itself, and even NACOLE, hoping for (like LeBron claims) some ACCOUNTABILITY. As of the writing of this book, all I've received is a very telling silence. For such a bunch of outspoken activists with no end of input for others, I guess I expected more.

Almost like I held them to a higher standard than the rest of society.

Unrealistic expectations abound, perhaps none more misplaced than the online cyberterrorist group, "Anonymous." They want their name to strike terror in any who oppose their demands, like petty muggers in an alleyway. At the very least, a message from Anonymous means your day just got worse. At the very most, it means your day can't get worse.

In August of 2014, St. Louis County Police Chief Jon Belmar got one of the latter messages. Earlier in the month, Michael Brown (18) was shot by Officer Darren Wilson after Brown attacked Wilson inside his police car and attempted to get the cop's gun. Two shots were fired inside the car, then ten more outside as Wilson pursued Brown on foot. Six shots struck Brown as he advanced on the officer, all in the front of his body. In Officer Wilson's own words, "Again, I don't recall how many times I hit him. I know at least once because he flinched again. At this point it looked like he was almost bulking up to run through the shots, like it was making him mad that I'm shooting at him." It was Wilson's first time firing his weapon on duty.[14]

However, according to protesters who weren't even present at the altercation, Wilson had not only murdered an innocent "boy," but he'd done it while shooting Brown in the back as he attempted to surrender. They staged protests both peaceful and violent, triggering a state of fear across the state. Understand, the St. Louis County Grand Jury later ruled to not indict Wilson, and the Department of Justice found forensic evidence that supported Wilson's report, concluding that Wilson had shot Brown in self-defense. In fact, Brown was shown on camera footage, three minutes before attacking Officer Wilson, stealing a box of cigars from the Ferguson Market and shoving the store clerk on his way out. Wilson, meanwhile, had just finished responding to a call regarding a baby with breathing problems.[15]

But the news doesn't give a shit about any of those details. Neither did the mob that rampaged through Missouri. Neither did Anonymous.

In the early hours before work, the cyberterrorists posted a picture of Police Chief Belmar's family home on Twitter, along with his address and personal phone number. That afternoon, another picture followed, this time of Belmar and his wife, along with the caption, "Nice photo, Jon. Your wife actually looks good for her age. Have you had enough?" Then another of someone inside his home, asleep on the couch. Then another of his wife and daughter. Anonymous told the Ferguson police department, "We are watching you very closely." They set up a website where they posted a video stating:

> If you abuse, harass — or harm in any way the
> protesters in Ferguson we will take every Web-based
> asset of your departments and governments off line.
> That is not a threat, it is a promise. If you attack the
> protesters, we will attack every server and computer
> you have. We will dox and release the personal
> information on every single member of the Ferguson
> Police Department, as well as any other jurisdiction
> that participates in the abuse. We will seize all your
> databases and E-Mail spools and dump them on the
> Internet. This is your only warning.

What did they want, you ask? This was before any court rulings
or investigation updates, and Chief Belmar hadn't released the
name of Darren Wilson as the officer who shot Brown. Why not?
Because the mob would have killed him. Anonymous, with all
their claims at power, didn't have that one bit of information they
wanted so that they could dox Wilson to the rioting crowds. They
threatened harm upon Belmar's family and wanted to do the same
to Wilson.

It didn't matter to Anonymous one way or the other, and they
carried through with the threat before awaiting a response. The
department fell into chaos, but Belmar succeeded in protecting
the life of his officer, and for that he deserves a commendation.
Anonymous, meanwhile, deserves to get dragged out into the light
like the scurrying rats they are and held accountable for the hatred
and anarchy they inserted into an already volatile situation.

Similar examples of doxing have happened in Portland,

Oregon, with the names, phone numbers, and home addresses of thirty-eight officers posted online, with captions urging protesters to go to these homes and enact vengeance for alleged misconduct and alleged brutality.[16]

More in Washington, DC, where hackers used a ransomware called "Babuk" to seize confidential police dossiers, which included personal information of some MPD officers gathered by HR.[17] In a climate where police are being executed in the street, identity theft pales in comparison to the threat of a home invasion from violent extremists.

When Googling Derek Chauvin's name (George Floyd's killer), the most popular autocomplete search results include:

- Derek Chauvin Trial
- * * Family
- * * Daughter
- * * kids
- * * case
- * * children
- * * wife
- * * parents

Some people might be honestly curious about the life of this cop who murdered someone on camera as he pressed his knee against Floyd's neck for almost nine minutes. But really? These searches aren't about familial curiosity; they're about revenge. I don't blame them for being angry about what happened, but these searches are about lashing out in rage for their misguided notion of justice. It's not justice to hunt down anyone's innocent loved ones, no matter how pissed off you might be.

Cyberstalking and cyberattacks are happening all across the country, to the degree that the Department of Homeland Security

(DHS) has issued a national warning to all police departments to anticipate direct attacks on officers' personal information at every level. Minneapolis, Kentucky, San Jose, New York… It's harder to find a list of departments that *haven't* been attacked. DHS recommends that officers take countermeasures to protect themselves, but that advice included things like "use two-step authentication" and "change your passwords often" and "don't take online quizzes." That input seems so incredibly weak compared with the damage that groups like Anonymous are capable of, and it's small comfort to rearrange passwords when you're afraid some psycho will track down the school your kids attend. Cops deserve better. My hope is that the FBI and DHS are growing more skilled at protecting our police officers' information from extremists, but it would be nice to see some evidence of that from time to time.

Clearly, our litigation regarding doxing is behind the times. The laws that hold doxers accountable for their actions are insufficient. If you post the personal information of another individual online with malicious intent, you should be held responsible for the threat you're making. In my mind, it's no different than positioning a knife for a clean stab. Your intent is to kill or maim another person (whether you convince someone else to do it for you or not) and, for that, you deserve to be in prison along with all the other degenerates.

CHAPTER EIGHT
GOT YOUR SIX

I started out on TikTok just out of sheer curiosity. It was gaining popularity and people were talking about it, hyping it up. I kept seeing TikTok videos shared on Instagram and Facebook, and I got on there just to play around with it. I wasn't familiar with it at first, of course, but I came across a lot of funny videos to scroll through and even some very educational videos. I thought, "Wow, TikTok is kind of great." Eventually, the infamous algorithm kicked in.

I started seeing other police officers posting videos and getting a pretty decent response from people, and I thought, "That's a good idea. I should throw my hat into the ring on this, because these cops are showing their true characters right on screen." There they were doing average, ordinary, everyday things like singing in the car on the way to work. Like regular people! Like they were humans.

This might be new information to a few but, occasionally during downtime at work, officers will dance around and act a fool to pass the time. I think that's good stuff for people to see. We're not all just sitting around a table stone-faced, thinking about how we can further violate someone's rights and reach our next bigotry merit badge. Cops "shoot the shit" and joke with each other. Sometimes it's that gallows humor, and sometimes it's pure nonsense just for the hell of it. And I thought TikTok would be a good way to show citizens that we're not all demons—not just that, but maybe if other cops saw some humor on the job, they might loosen up a bit and drop the Lawbot act. I found #humanizethebadge and saw that a lot of TikTokers had beaten me to the punch.

And I was thrilled.

I wanted to be a part of it, to help people understand that police officers are not these machines that they're made out to be; they're people who have compassion for others. They have personalities. They have senses of humor. They have hobbies and other interests outside of law enforcement. The videos showed that they don't just care about police work; there are other things in their lives that help identify them as individuals with hearts and minds and personalities.

I decided to jump on board, so I started making TikToks. The first few I made didn't have anything to do with police work; they were just baby steps on a new social platform. But then I tried a few in my uniform and started getting great responses from every direction. I gained more and more followers from people liking, sharing, and commenting on my videos. It wasn't just the entertainment value; it was a public response to seeing something they'd never seen before: a cop in uniform behaving like a person. From there, the popularity just kept increasing and increasing. A few of the videos went viral. You may have seen one in particular regarding a certain celebrity running his mouth where it doesn't belong.

I never anticipated that this one video would take my life to this point. I mean, here you are reading my book, for shit sakes. How does that happen to a guy from Idaho?

But, as seems to always happen, someone took offense.

Complaints came in to the Bellevue PD where I was working as a deputy marshal, accusing me of racism and defaming my uniform, and it didn't take long for them to hand me a suspension without pay. So I went home, and I soon found out that my close friend, Gannon Ward, had started a GoFundMe campaign to recoup my lost wages. As it turns out, people felt for my situation, and donations skyrocketed. Thousands of people gave their money to the cause, far more than necessary to cover my unpaid suspension, but the amount just kept climbing. Messages from total strangers rolled past that said things like, "We love you, Nate!" and "This money is for you! Don't give it away!" For the first time in my life, I thought about things like being debt-free and feeling secure about my daughter's future. I'd never been so humbled in my life. To sit there and watch those dollars pile on, especially in this fucked-up economy, was a splash of ice water to my face. Here was my wake-up call. Because they weren't just donating to some poor schlub who got behind on his bills; they were donating to a cop who had dared to speak out and got silenced for it. They were donating because I had opened my mouth rather than shutting it.

I had to do something with this opportunity.

While I got some gears turning on the idea for a nonprofit to help cops like me, the Bellevue PD received *hundreds* of email complaints on my behalf—but not cop-hate like you might expect. No, these complaints expressed displeasure that the higher-ups had suspended me for calling out LeBron James' idiocy regarding Nicholas Reardon. Turns out people didn't care for the department's ruling. A whole lot of people.

I stopped by the office to sign for something unrelated, and there it was: a stack of printed emails the length of my forearm, all protesting the decision to punish me for utilizing my First Amendment rights in a non-harmful, non-toxic, non-confrontational, hilarious manner. I'm still working my way through them, but the best estimate the other officers could give me was at least two reams of paper—well over a thousand messages. I can't begin to describe what it felt like to see the sheer physicality of all that irrefutable evidence saying I had the support of enough people to make a difference. That level of affirmation was a head rush, and it just further cemented the drive within me to keep pushing back against all the bullshit that's been piling up against police officers for decades.

To the side of those thousand-plus emails supporting me was a tiny pile of papers: the emails from those who agreed with my suspension and wished me ill, those who insisted I never come back to work, and so forth. There were six negative emails in total.

My path was clear.

Bellevue sat me down to discuss my return to work. With my attorney once again present, I signed a "Last Chance Agreement" that allowed me to resume my shifts, but stated in no uncertain terms that the department would find a way to fire me in the very near future. I could go back to work if I didn't step a toe out of line, including a stipulation that I not make any more TikToks.

Well, I made more TikToks. And I got fired. Again. One could say I'm pretty good at getting fired and not so good at keeping my constitutionally protected opinions to myself. One could.

I started receiving an influx of goodwill from people all over the country (and several outside it). My social media blew up. Between Facebook, Instagram, and TikTok, I received over fifteen hundred private messages within just a few days. Followers, Likes, and contacts soared. I started getting interview requests for local news stations, radio stations, and podcasts.

My personal email flooded with over a thousand messages from supporters, all saying how much they agreed with my stance and my right to speak. I got physical checks in the mail, sometimes in ten- or twenty-dollar amounts (some much more). People sent letters and greeting cards with cash and little notes of encouragement inside. It wasn't all money, but the outpouring of generosity meant so much more to me anyway.

"Back the Blue."

"Thanks for speaking out."

"You said what all of us were thinking."

"Got your six, brother."

And they just kept coming.

I recognize that I'd be in dire straits today without each of these amazing Americans. I want to share with you just a small sampling of the goodness directed at me, and I'll let their words speak for them. My sincere apologies for not being able to include military or law enforcement ranks in the credits; we had to remove them to protect identities. Consider this the beginning of my own database, one that sheds light on the real truth of police officers around the country. We are not the monsters that some would make us out to be. If you recognize your own message here, this is my way of saying, "Thank you."

"Dear Chief, It is with a sad heart that I write you this email. First of all, I am not one to go out of my way to write to individuals if I don't agree with them or with their actions or points of view. I have always been one to stand on the sidelines and respect everyone's opinions and actions. But not today. At a time when our country is completely being destroyed by extremists with extreme points of view, you decide to side with them and place one of your officers on leave for voicing his opinion. I feel sorry for all the men and women in uniform who work under you. It must be horrible to have to go to work each day knowing their Chief will bend over backwards for the angry mob. I hope these brave men and women come to their senses and realize they have zero support from their department. I hope they leave your department in flocks and find departments with backbones who are willing to side with what is right, not with the angry mob. I truly feel you know what you did was wrong, but you still gave in and sided with the people who are trying to destroy everything you've worked so hard for your entire life. It is only a matter of time that the angry mob will turn on you, the same way you turned on Officer Silvester. They will stop at nothing, nothing you do or say will make them happy. They will do everything to destroy your career, that's what happens when you side with the mob instead of actual reason and rationale. They don't care about you, they just care about destroying the police."

-Joanna F., America

"The country is watching how administrations are handling police officer suspensions and misconduct. While it's common in the past for activists to be coming from one side, please realize that the other side of reality is becoming involved and will no longer tolerate political correctness and spineless administrators to punish cops that have done NOTHING wrong. I am sure you are nice people and just trying to do what seems right, but now people like me that don't normally say anything are forced to say something."

-Michael F., Arizona

"As a retired Law Enforcement Officer and Chief of Police, I am astonished at the lack of support you have chosen to show all Law

Enforcement Officers of this great nation. The action you chose to take... show that you had no plan but a knee jerk reaction. Poor leadership qualities. You have just put several more blocks in the wall weakness is putting between society and Law Enforcement...You know as well as I this will be looked at for years and taught in leadership conferences as how NOT to support your officers. Hopefully your leadership will soon be replaced by people who know how to tear walls down instead of the cowards building them. Strong Letter To Follow."

-Mike F., Illinois

"What Deputy Silvester did was not only commendable, but necessary. We have to push back on this narrative that police are racist killers. Sadly everyday, the police go to work with targets on their back, and for Deputy Silvester to show the courage in showing the ridiculous and dangerous rhetoric that incites the violence against police officers every day, he should be receiving a medal, not facing discipline. Shame on the Marshal's Office for even considering it because of a citizen complaint. If we don't stop appeasing these fools, it is never going to end."

-Suzanne N., Ohio

"Lebron James sucks - your officer spoke the mind of millions. Lebron James is racist and does nothing to unify America, but rather divides it. Don't apologize for your officer, grow a spine and stop caring so much about what whiny liberals say. Give him a promotion for exercising his first amendment right - (ya'll believe in that right)?"

- Sam B., America

"What you've done to Officer Silvester is absolutely abhorrent. LeBron James literally put a target on the backs of young men and women all across our country, and the leaders of our law enforcement agencies are all cowering in a corner, too afraid to even respond. Meanwhile, your employees and colleagues are dying in the street due to lack of leadership...No wonder cops are quitting in record numbers. Surely this will help you recruit future peacekeepers, right?"

-A Concerned Citizen, America

"The reasonable thing to do is to drop the issue, ignore the noise from for-profit pot-stirrers, and side with your community over those who despise you, your city, and your country."

-Deryk W., Idaho

"Chief, I am a retired officer in Texas. I saw Officer Silvester's video and in my opinion, he did nothing wrong...I thought he was a very funny comedian. When I discovered he was a LEO, my thought was "well done." When I found out he had been suspended, I felt anger and disappointment. I understand the position you are in, given the political climate we live in but we need to return our society to sanity. We need you to have the courage to do the right thing."

-Pat S., Texas

"The whole country is aware of this terrible war on the police. A target has been put on their backs by the media, by Hollywood, and big mouthed uninformed sports stars such as LeBron James. They say terrible things and make untrue accusations all day everyday, yet the police cannot respond in a non-threatening way? You need to have your officers backs. Personally I'm not sure why anybody would ever become a police officer in today's climate, and instead of supporting your officers you suspend one for speaking the absolute truth."

-Leslie G., New Hampshire

"I do not see why he was disciplined for a video that hurt nobody, and even provided some humor during a time where there is so much hate. It is a shame that this officer puts his life on the line every time he goes out on a call, yet his own administration will not support him...I hope whoever is responsible for his suspension will rectify the situation, and continue to work WITH our police forces, not AGAINST."

-Jonathan L., California

"I understand I do not live within your jurisdiction...However, before matriculating to law school and going on to a successful law practice 27 years ago, I was a deputy sheriff...and as a former law enforcement officer (not to mention the father of a police officer for a Metro-Atlanta, GA agency), I hope you will take under consideration this email in support of Dep. Silvester.

I do not need to tell you that law enforcement is an incredibly challenging occupation these days. It requires split-second, often life-or-death decisions but then subjects the decision maker's actions to retrospective reviews where often the "evidence" is a cell phone video that was initiated only **after** the actions that precipitated the citizen contact. Given that the Columbus incident was not one such case and that the entirety of the officer's actions and interactions were recorded, I thought cooler heads would prevail and this would quickly be viewed as a tragic event, one that was the direct and proximate result of Ms. Bryant's conduct. So naturally I was a bit shocked when that did not turn out to be the case. Instead, celebrities like Mr. James and news outlets painted this as yet another instance of "White cop shoots Black citizen." Virtually no one spoke up about how the officer's quick decisions and marksmanship saved one young woman from the irrational and imminently harmful actions of another young woman.

That lack of any defense was a tragedy in itself and your deputy tried to address and rectify that shortcoming by using humor and sarcasm to show just how ludicrous things have become; when a completely justifiable, reasonable, judicious and authorized use of force was turned on its head and used to malign the Columbus officer in particular and law enforcement officers in general, your deputy tried to add a little perspective. That voice should be supported, not punished."

-B.H., Washington

"Your leadership is the reason so many officers, good officers, are leaving their called professions and trades behind. You don't support them and your so fearful of being called a racist that you don't recognize the truth when its right in front of you."

-Diane M., America

"Please back your officer. This witch hunt Against Cops has to be stopped...Back your Cops."

-Ray D., Idaho

"Shame on you for suspending Deputy Silvester. No wonder people can't defend the police, when their own employers CHOOSE to not support them."

-Angie M., Illinois

"I RARELY contact law enforcement about anything negative because I support you THAT MUCH. However, suspending Nate Silvester is absolutely **asinine**. That's the kind of Deputy Marshal I want on my block and in my neighborhood...Deputy Marshal Silvester used clever tongue-in-cheek to call out the evil being spewed by an ignorant, arrogant, clueless, destructive basketball player whose words are **incredibly dangerous** to the community en masse. And who do you defend? The basketball player! By suspending Deputy Silvester, you've told the world, "the basketball player should be able to spew **stupidity** and **threats** with no recourse." LeBron James, in essence, said "attack a police officer" with his tweets. And instead of defending those in law enforcement, you suspend one of your own? That's a swing and a massive miss."

-John M., America

"You say your town is the top 50 safest cities around??? ITS BECAUSE OF GREAT POLICE OFFICERS LIKE THE ONE YOU ARE PUNISHING FOR FINALY SPEAKING UP AGAINST THE BULLSHIT CANCEL CULTURE MOVIE STARS AND THE BULLSHIT REVERSE RACISM THERE PUTTING OUR OFFICERS THROUGH!!!"

-Anthony C., America

"As a 24-year military veteran myself, I applaud the spirit and pride exhibited by your officer in his recent satire. His willingness to insert some humor into our otherwise staid and concerning times is a welcome respite from the political nightmare in which we find ourselves. As the department's leader, you should be proud of such public servants. I can only imagine how difficult it must be to find and retain men and women willing to serve in today's climate."

-Byron T., America

"I am writing you from Canada to express my support for Deputy Marshal Silvester's video on tic tok. He should have the support of all good police officers and honest citizens. As good officers it is time that you fight all hatred. He fought hate in a non-violent way and should be commended."

-Mike W., Canada

"Why was deputy marshal Silvester suspended? Do officers not deserve to have a first amendment? Is a basketball player more important to you than your own staff? Is any famous person feelings more important? Why don't you work on actual police reform rather than suspending or firing your own staff just because that's what the media says to do? This is a disgrace to see. Someone who is calling out the media for their lies and their assault on police across the US is suspended rather than praised for having the guts to actually say something about it...We want, no, we need more officers like Deputy Marshal Silvester."

-Brian G., America

"Good evening Mayor Ned,

Just wanted to drop you a line and tell you that I spoke with my wife and we agreed to cancel our travel plans to come to your city this summer with our family because of your treatment of officer Nate Silvester.

Frankly speaking Mayor Ned, I also wanted you to know that I just sent a certified letter to the CEO of Coldwell Banker Ryan Gorman to advise him that I will no longer consider doing business with Coldwell Banker for either my personal nor my company Real estate transactions because they have someone like you representing them. Considering my Extensive financial portfolio as well as my prior dealings with Coldwell Banker, I think Ryan Corman will take my letter seriously.

You see Mayor Ned, using your new found position as mayor to push your left wing cancel culture has opened the eyes of military veteran business owners such as myself so as to smarten up and take our business somewhere else.

In short Mayor Ned, taking advantage of my first amendment right that I earned whilst serving as a United States Marine, I wanted to be the first to tell you to go pound sand right up your ass and think twice the next time you attempt to subvert another Americans constitutional rights!

In closing, I plan on donating to whoever runs against you as well as others on the city council in your next election cycle as I've placed that date on my calendar. You see Mayor Ned, the best part about being a someone of self made financial means is that it feels great to donate to worthy causes just like I did today when I donated to officer Nate Silvester gofund me account!" -Scott D., America

"Officer Nate Silvester deserves a free speech award for making fun of LeBron James. His humor cast a positive, thoughtful, and intelligent response to the insanity spewed from LeBron James. In fact, it portrayed your office in a very positive light by employing intelligent and thoughtful officers who clearly know right from wrong. The genius of the First Amendment is that the powerful cannot (Even though they try to) control the narrative. This is a government designed to be of the people, by the people, and for the people. We should never restrict or cancel speech, particularly speech that reflects the truth and diminishes the corrupt narratives of powerful people. That is freedom."

-John V., Massachusetts

CHAPTER NINE
LIFE AFTER TIKTOK

How was I supposed to know it was gonna go mega-viral? I ask that facetiously but, in all reality, there was no way anyone could have anticipated that the "LeBron TikTok," as it were, was going to get the reaction it did. Yeah, it was funny. I like to laugh just like anyone else, so I slathered it with sarcasm in an effort to mock the NBA superstar for his self-proclaimed policing expertise while simultaneously making the viewers laugh. It worked—with some people. I can't pinpoint exactly why my video stood out among fifty other videos I'd seen other officers do mocking LeBron James for his over-involvement. For whatever reason, it did, and it caught people's attention all around the world.

That video struck a couple different chords. On one hand, I acted out the exact thing everyone else "on my side" was thinking, and there was thunderous applause in the form of Likes, shares, comments, letters, emails, private messages, interview requests, and donations. People from countries like Scotland, Mexico, Canada, Australia, and the UK reached out to tell me how much they admired me for standing up to the "woke" social justice warriors that we have the displeasure of hearing from daily. As it turns out, there are quite a large number of people (a quiet majority, if you will) who still have the ability to reason and think critically and who are huge supporters of law enforcement. They understand the metaphor of the thin blue line. To paraphrase a quote from George Orwell, "We sleep peacefully at night because of those men and women who stand ready to do violence on our behalf." I know that's not the exact quote, but it's the exact intent of it. The people who understand this know the reality of the world we live in. There are violent aggressors in our midst who can't be reasoned with, no matter the issue. Their own self-interests and tendency toward violence outweigh the common good and whatever compassion they have for other human beings, if any. The thin blue line—the police—is what separates the offender from the prospective victim. Those would-be victims are grateful for the men and women who wear the badge and keep the wolves at bay so that they can live peaceful lives.

The other chord I struck was with the woke crowd. I never intended for my message to be overtly political, yet support for law enforcement has become a partisan issue, and those on the other side of the aisle did not take kindly to my criticism of their spokesperson, the self-appointed "King James." This included my own mayor, Ned Burns, and the city council of Bellevue, Idaho. They jumped right on that cancel culture bandwagon and called for my termination. Mind you, I posted the video to TikTok on Saturday, April 24th, 2021 at around 10:00 a.m. By the following evening I was receiving text messages and phone calls from friends and family members who were seeing my video played on the news and reading articles about it. Sadly, the first question posed to me was, "Is this going to affect your job?"

"Well, it shouldn't," I said. "They didn't have a problem with any of my other videos."

It's unfortunate that we're in such a state regarding law enforcement that my non-police friends know the danger of an officer receiving media attention that isn't sanctioned by the chief of police. I was speaking out on behalf of law enforcement officers in a show of solidarity, specifically with Officer Reardon from Columbus, Ohio. Why would my support offend anyone? What harm could that video possibly do to my community, or any community?

As it turns out, it doesn't have to make sense. The "offense" doesn't have to be harmful or illegal; it just has to be contrary to the narrative of the Left, which it definitely was. So they were out for blood.

The following Monday, I spoke with the mayor and asked him what exactly his issue with my video was. He explained to me that he'd received complaints from a couple Bellevue citizens who expressed that they no longer felt safe in their own town and couldn't trust me to do my job.

"Are you fucking kidding me?" was my response. "How on earth does a satirical video, the main premise of which is to support law enforcement, in any way indicate that I'm incapable or incompetent to do police work?" Now, if Mayor Ned actually had a set of testicles, his answer would have been, "It doesn't, but someone disliked what you had to say and it offends our Leftist sensibilities." Not that it would have excused anything, but I could have at least respected him for being honest.

Initially, my marshal (boss) had my back. She recruited me, after all, and knew how good I was at my job. She knew my experience was valuable to the agency and didn't want me gone. She tried to reason with the mayor and city council and succeeded in saving my job, for the time being. I was suspended for a week without pay. That's when things got interesting.

My best friend of twenty-six years, Gannon, created the GoFundMe campaign that would help me recover the wages I was going to lose for that week. He was irate that my department would suspend me over the TikTok video. A few hours after Gannon published the campaign, I checked the status and noticed that about six hundred dollars had been donated. "Wow, that's so generous of those donors!" I thought to myself. A few hours after that, a co-worker of mine called and asked if I was aware of the GoFundMe. I thought, "How does he know about it already?" So I went online and checked.

Gannon had originally set the goal for the campaign at ten thousand dollars. He thought that was a lofty goal (and I agreed), but went for it anyway. The donations were up to six thousand dollars. I was shocked. People were being so generous and compassionate towards me, but why? People lose their jobs every day; what made me so special? Why was this so important to some that they would donate this amount of money to me? Pretty soon the campaign reached one hundred thousand dollars. My jaw was on the floor. Was I dreaming? At the same time the donations were flooding in, I was receiving interview requests from very notable news networks like Fox News, CNN, Blaze TV, and Newsmax, to name a few. Outlets like *The Gateway Pundit* and *Newsweek* had already done articles on my story featuring my TikTok video.

Now, if you haven't seen the video, imagine me as a police officer rolling up to a disturbance where two people are fighting; one person has a knife and is about to stab the other. Before taking action I call LeBron James to ask him what exactly I should do. After learning that both parties involved are Black, LeBron instructs me not to get involved since deadly force is justified and he doesn't want a white cop shooting another Black person. During the pretend phone call, I explain how his logic doesn't make much sense but, because he's a superstar basketball player, he must know what he's talking about. I drive away, leaving the two people to work it out on their own. It was a sixty-second video. As far as I've been able to estimate, the video was viewed over ten million times across social media and mainstream media. Sean Hannity described it as "funny and totally on the mark."

But still, why? Why the windfall? Why so many donations? Well, when the letters, emails, and messages started to flow in, I figured it out.

Some people donated because, for whatever reason, they generally support law enforcement and saw this as an opportunity to show it; others donated because I got suspended and the threat of termination loomed. But the main reason people supported me was because I stood up to the woke mob. I said what a lot of others were afraid to, especially other officers. I spoke out against the scourge of radical ideologies that have plagued our country in recent years and exposed a serious flaw in the argument against police and their use of deadly force, and I did it with a combination of humor and indiscretion towards the insufferable rhetoric from the radical Left that has been force-fed to us on a daily basis. I said exactly what so many people were thinking and feeling.

Does this mean that those other people were cowards for not speaking out? No. You put yourself at risk when you share an opinion that doesn't align with the Left. I don't blame anyone for not sticking their necks out and putting their livelihoods at stake, because these people will take everything they can get and still call it insufficient.

Make no mistake: when the cancel culture comes for you, they come for it all. They want your career, your savings, your home, and even your life. That's not to say they will come kill you but, in my case, I was "encouraged" to kill myself many times. With all the support rolling in also came the letters, calls, and emails to my department demanding my termination and demanding criminal charges be filed. For what crime? I don't know. They demanded the GoFundMe campaign be canceled and, since it wasn't, they demanded I pay the money back or donate it all, because I didn't deserve it. They demanded lawsuits be filed against me, and for what offense? I still don't know. I've been labeled a racist, a bigot, a fraud, a scam artist, and a murderer. People with ample time on their hands actually made copies of my previously posted TikToks and dubbed racial slurs into them, then shared them as if they were sharing an original video of mine. Interesting how they were motivated to craft such machinations after watching a sixty-second video of me making fun of a basketball player.

If you're seething with anger at this point, or even just a little miffed, it's very understandable. You see, the people demanding the GoFundMe be canceled never donated to it, yet feel entitled to dictate what happened with the money that was donated. People who didn't even live in the community where I policed demanded I be terminated. Members of the self-proclaimed "Party of Tolerance and Inclusivity" wanted my very existence to cease, simply because I disagreed with them. This is the same group of people that so many police administrators cower to when the pressure is put on them to discipline an officer for saying something online as innocuous as "All lives matter."

Cancel culture is a dangerous thing, a thing that scares even the best police officers, and for good reason. When I came back to work after my weeklong suspension, a few officers from neighboring agencies reached out to me. They asked if we could meet and talk in private, which we did, in empty parking lots. I acted out of curiosity; why the hush-hush attitude? They simply wanted to tell me how much they appreciated and agreed with what I had to say. They wished they could have said what I did. They wished they didn't have to tell me they had my back in such a private setting. But these guys have families who rely on them. They have benefits, a pension, and a steady paycheck, which could all be stripped from them should the wrong person hear them say out loud, "I support Nate." That's how powerful and malicious cancel culture is. Look at all the sneaking around in *1984* and tell me you don't draw any connections. It's scary as fuck out here.

I was eating lunch with a few off-duty cops one day. One of them shares a joint Facebook account with his wife. His wife is a fan of mine and shares many of my posts. This officer told me he had to instruct his wife to add her own signature at the end of each shared post so no one would think he was the one sharing them. This was my friend here!

If this is all starting to sound like utter madness to you, good. That's exactly what it is. How did we get to the point where an officer can't show his support for another officer whose platform is humanizing the badge?

I've frequently been asked regarding the TikTok, "Do you regret it?" I've answered this question the same way every time:

"NO!"

Even my supporters probably think I'm a little bit crazy. Putting my job on the line, and losing it, in order to simply speak my mind seems unfathomable to most. But something has to give. Someone has to stand up for what's right. We can't just sit back until we're all canceled into submission and have conformed to a perverted social justice agenda. I had a choice to make. I could tuck my tail between my legs, keep my mouth shut, and possibly salvage my job as a deputy marshal in Bellevue, Idaho. Or, I could maintain my integrity and fight for what I know is right. I ask myself regularly if what I have to say is important to other people. Is this battle worthwhile? Will it make a difference? Well, many other people have answered that for me. Officers and civilians alike have reached out over the months to say things like:

"Don't back down! We need your voice!"

"Keep fighting the good fight, brother."

"Don't let them silence you!"

"Thank you for saying what we all wanted to."

"You should seriously consider running for office."

Taking into consideration all the support I've been getting, along with how hard the opposition has been trying to silence me, maybe what I have to say is important after all. If I have the opportunity to affect some lasting change in this country, then that is my new duty.

I love police work. I was good at it. I can hold my head high knowing I made a difference in the communities I served and in the lives of individuals I met. But I can't continue to speak out against corruption and wokeism if I'm constrained by a policy that is written to protect administrators and cut officers off at the knee. I'm now free to speak my mind as loudly as I see fit without the looming threat of unemployment, which would inevitably result from some vindictive social justice warrior taking issue with a photo or video I posted on social media depicting me wearing the thin-blue-line patch. Now, I can cover myself from head to toe in the thin-blue-line flag, and there's not a chief or mayor or city council person that can do a damn thing about it.

Digressing slightly, when I was put on suspension, the mayor of Bellevue, Idaho, instructed the marshal's office to remove the thin-blue-line patch that we'd all proudly displayed before. He believed that officers who wear the patch couldn't be objective and fair in their enforcement of the law. The symbol isn't new. The history of the thin-blue-line concept dates back to the Crimean War, when it was actually the "thin red line," symbolizing a line of British soldiers who held off a Russian cavalry charge. It was adopted by the United States Army in the 1900s as they marched into battle wearing their blue uniforms. It wasn't until the 1950s when the phrase and the flag became mainstream in symbolizing the courage and sacrifice shown by law enforcement officers in protecting the American people. Those who actually stand for its true, original message shouldn't be considered incompetent or untrustworthy of performing police work in a fair and just manner.

Maybe one day the Left will explain it all to us. Until then, the typical parroted slogans of "Defund the police" and "Fuck Blue Lives Matter" are the best we're gonna get.

When I was interviewed for my job at the Bellevue Marshal's Office, the mayor and two city council members were on the panel of interviewers. I was asked very clearly and plainly what my political affiliation was. After explaining that I have a conservative political perspective, it was made clear to me that Blaine County, Idaho, is a blue county in a red state. I was then asked if my political beliefs would interfere with my ability to police residents who don't share the same beliefs. My reply was that politics and law enforcement should have nothing to do with each other. Looking back, maybe I should have shouted it from the rooftops. The law is very black-and-white (not Black-vs-white!). Judicial proceedings are their own animal, but the duty of an officer is to enforce our laws without passion or prejudice, irrespective of political affiliation, race, gender, sexual orientation, or religious preference.

But then I wondered, will these elected officials have a problem with me? Why would they even ask that question? Isn't it illegal to ask that due to discrimination? (Matter of fact, it is). Then the mayor asked, "What are your thoughts on implicit bias in policing?" What a loaded question. I explained to the mayor that I have never treated anyone differently in my personal or professional life based on the color of their skin, and I'd never seen any other officer I'd worked with do it either. I further explained that all the information I'd read on implicit bias testing was inconsistent and unreliable, and is another fallacy used by "certain groups" to push an agenda that I vehemently disagree with. His look was of utter shock. Apparently, no one had ever been that honest with him before.

I couldn't help but be totally appalled at this point. The mayor attended my interview wearing a flannel shirt, corduroy pants, and sandals while I had shown up in my best suit and tie, and this smug asshole had the audacity to disparage my chosen profession, along with all the good men and women doing the job, with accusations of bias and discrimination.

Fuck you, Ned, I thought to myself. It's always the ones who've never worn the badge—or have any realistic idea of what police work is like—who are the most critical.

My marshal and I kept in regular contact. We didn't work much together because there was only one of us on duty at a time, but we had lunch together one day during my suspension. She was worried I might quit because of all the heat I was getting from the mayor and city attorney. She explained that after I was served my letter of discipline, the city attorney later contacted her and told her to order me to take down all of my videos on social media that depicted me in my police uniform.

Here's something not many people understand: my TikToks were all done while I was either on a break or while I was off duty (imagine such a thing existing). I never disclosed the name of my agency in any of my videos and didn't pretend to represent the views or opinions of my agency.

"Not going to happen," I replied. "If that's what they wanted, they should have put it in their letter of discipline. I signed that letter days before this conversation and that ship has sailed. You can fire me if you want, but those videos have brought some much-needed positivity into the law enforcement world and I'm not taking them down."

Some of you may be thinking, *It's no wonder he lost his job with how defiant and impudent he was.* Perhaps you're right, but when was the last time a conformist ever accomplished anything noteworthy? Don't get me wrong; I understand the importance of workplace discipline and the employer/employee relationship. But if there is an injustice that needs to be remedied, it's the way police officers have been treated in this country the last few years. I'm not about to back down from that fight when I'm in the vanguard. If any administrators (i.e. chiefs, captains, lieutenants) are reading this right now, how underhanded do you have to be to demand loyalty, honesty, and accountability from your rank-and-file officers, only to slam the door on them as the mob marches into town demanding their heads? I know not all administrators are like this, but I've worked for some and I know a lot of others have, too. We're seeing a pattern of chiefs, mayors, and commissioners all over the country kowtowing to the woke crowd. District attorneys are using officers as sacrificial lambs, charging them with crimes to avoid riots and looting, in cases where the officers were justified. Google Betty Shelby. How is this okay? Why are we letting this stand? Because you typically don't hear about it, until recently. Out of sight, out of mind.

Many administrators in the upper echelons of their respective agencies have no supervision or oversight. There is no one above them putting them in check to ensure they're treating their employees in a consistently fair, objective manner. They're handed the keys to the kingdom and given free reign. Sweeping decisions directly affecting police officers and their families literally come down to, "Well, let me step into Jim's office and see what he thinks." They selectively enforce policies when the mood hits them and, if you make it onto their shit list, your days are numbered. They WILL find a reason to fire you, and they will be looking for that reason diligently.

All the intra-office drama aside, these are the same types of administrators that will cave under the pressure of the mob looking to ruin the life of a police officer. They give great pep talks during shift briefings about how they value their officers and understand what a difficult and important job they have to do, and how the officers are "the tip of the spear" and blah blah blah. But when they perceive the slightest hint of danger to their six-figure salaries (which citizens pay for), all those morals, principles, and scruples they preach to you go right out the window, and they will lead you to the slaughter themselves for something as harmless as saying "Back the Blue" on a Facebook post—all because "Karen" doesn't believe an officer of the law should post something that denotes bias (in her opinion). Is Karen welcome to her opinion, just as much as I am? Of course. Are administrators allowed to ruin lives over it? Apparently, sadly, wrongly, yes.

We've seen a lot of this in the news media in 2020 and 2021. As of the writing of this book, a group of DC police officers are currently being investigated by their department after an interaction with a citizen who was recording their exchange on his phone, and he was there with a mission. These officers were in the normal course of their duties when the citizen started pestering them, trying to get them to say something offensive. The voice behind the camera asked, "Ya'll gonna kill me like Ma'Khia Bryant?" To which one of the officers replied, "You gonna stab somebody like her?".[18] The officer who said it hasn't yet been identified and it's hard to tell from the video which officer said it because they were all wearing face coverings. But why the fuck does it matter, and what do you think they're going to do with that information? Why is the DC Metro Police Department wasting time investigating this? The officer answered this guy's question in a very straightforward way: don't try to stab people and you won't get shot by the police. Common sense, right? Well, common sense has no place in the narrative that ALL cops are evil, racist bigots with itchy trigger fingers. And the DC MPD is buying into that narrative at the expense of the taxpayers. We're losing good cops because of it.

Imagine applying for or being recruited into a police agency. Typically, a recruiter will sugarcoat the job description by leaving out the truth, because it's getting harder and harder to fill those shift slots. What if he told you exactly how it was going to be?

"We're going to start you out at really low pay. Sixteen bucks an hour should do it. Then we'll put you on probation for a year. That way, if you do anything we don't like, we can just fire you without any sort of due process. Right-to-work state; you understand. You'll alternate between day shift and night shift every couple of months so you don't get too used to either. This is going to mess with your sleep cycle, so be prepared to come to work tired every day, which really amps up the internal stress levels. You'll be expected to handle calls involving, but not limited to: the removal of crying children from the squalor they live in with drug-addicted parents; examining the dead body of someone who just put a shotgun in his mouth and blew his brains all over the living room, then interviewing his twelve-year-old son who found him that way; finally, you'll also get into a foot pursuit with a wanted felon who may pull a gun on you or anyone else, and has done so before, so you'll need to remember to run *toward* the bullets. You'll have about a split second to decide whether or not deadly force is justified. If you're right, nice job, I guess. If you're wrong, you go to prison. Oh, and that should all happen by the end of your first week.

"When can you start?"

'*Where do I fucking sign?*' is what you're thinking, right? No? Did that raise some red flags for you? If it didn't make you hesitate at least a little, either reread that thing or maybe look into some counseling of your own.

The reality police officers face today is that they're expected to deal with the bullets, the blood, and the brutality all without a change in comportment. They're required to have an attorney's understanding of their respective states' statutes and city ordinances. They study case law to keep up on how those decisions made by the courts will affect their future enforcement action. They maintain their certifications by completing at least forty hours of training per year, but most officers train a lot more than that, and at their own expense. Many of them also enroll in school during their careers to better themselves and to improve the quality of service they deliver to the taxpayers. But all of that counts for nothing when any self-proclaimed expert in policing calls the chief to complain about how they think an officer should have done his or her job. That person's opinion carries more weight than all of the blood, sweat, and tears an officer has poured into his or her career, and that's the bullshit that has to be stopped.

Does any of this seem fair or reasonable? Some of you may think so because you pay taxes, right? You pay taxes, so you have the right to dictate how officers do their jobs, right? Well, when you go to the hospital for surgery—a surgery you will pay through the nose for—do you tell the surgeon how to do the procedure? I certainly hope not. Oh, by the way, officers pay taxes, too. You heard me. How much of your medical bill does your surgeon cover?

During a deadly force incident, officers today are faced with the quandary: "If I pull the trigger to stop the crime, even if I'm justified, I'll likely lose my job. The district attorney will charge me with a crime to avoid civil unrest. I'll lose the means with which I care for my family. I'll be vilified by the media and labeled a racist or a thug. I'll have to start over completely, assuming I don't go to prison. Or, if I don't pull the trigger, this person could kill me where I stand, or kill someone else." That's a whole lot to have on your mind when the assailant is reaching for a concealed weapon.

So, to avoid having to make that choice, officers are quitting. Why the hell would they want to stay? At the time of writing this book, police officers in cities like Atlanta and Seattle are literally walking off the job. The entire riot team with the Portland Police Department up and quit. I don't blame them one bit! If you keep biting the hand that feeds you, you'll eventually starve. If you keep labeling criminals as victims and cops as criminals, eventually you'll have no one to keep the actual criminals at bay.

I've often been asked, "Where are you going from here?" or

"Are you going to get another law enforcement job?" After heavy consideration, I can say my answer is no, even though I've been offered several positions by many agencies across the country. At this point, I've been given a stage from which I can broadcast my message: the message of accountability and culture reform. We hear the typical slogans of "police reform," "defund the police," and "de-escalation training for cops" over and over. However, if we keep misidentifying the problem we'll never find the solution.

The problem is not systemic racism or corrupt cops.

Again, please don't add fuel to the fire by misquoting me. I know there are bad actors in the law enforcement field, just as there are in any profession. There are pockets of evil and racism in our country, but that doesn't equate to a systemic failure. Those people are INDIVIDUALS who represent a fraction of the population. They're not even whole apples. For years and years, police officers have received the proper training for de-escalating volatile situations, crisis intervention training, and verbal compliance.

The problem that has been misidentified by opponents and critics of law enforcement is that people are being unjustifiably shot by police. According to critics, these unjustified shootings are a symptom of two root causes: police brutality and racism.

This is why we're spinning our wheels. The elephant in the room no one wants to address, the real cause, is cultural dysfunction. There is a culture in our country that perpetuates the victim mentality. It instills in people a sense of entitlement that the rules do not apply to them, that there shouldn't be any repercussions for their criminal behavior, that they have the right to break laws and then resist arrest and fight with the police. That being held accountable for their crimes is the result of a flawed, unjust system, and they are being targeted for something other than their criminality, whether it's the color of their skin, their socio-economic status, or their sexual orientation. Ronald Reagan said it best: "We must reject the idea that every time a law's broken, society is guilty rather than the lawbreaker. It is time to restore the American precept that each individual is accountable for his actions."

But it's much easier to blame someone or something else for our poor choices. Acknowledging that this cultural dysfunction is the root cause means there is a lot of work to be done by individuals, and there is no amount of government intervention or spending that can fix it. That work has to be done in the home by the parents.

Most of these incidents of police shootings we see are the end result of the failure of parents to teach morals, respect, accountability, and decency to their children. Many of these children later become adults with a lack of respect for authority and a predilection for crime. Yet, after years of terrible parenting and poor decision-making, it's somehow the fault of the cop who is called to deal with the man who is threatening his girlfriend with a gun, or a knife, or a syringe.

So, my future in law enforcement is going to have to wait, or maybe that chapter of my life is over. Right now, I can't squander an opportunity to fight for my brothers and sisters in blue who have been silenced by lopsided policies, administrators, elected officials, and mainstream media, and who shouldn't have to choose between their principles and their livelihoods, but are forced to anyway. They deserve better for the sacrifices they have to make in order to protect a community and a country that doesn't deserve them.

CHAPTER TEN
CHANGING MINDS

I was going to call this chapter "Changing the Narrative," but "the narrative" today is something that a large group of people can fabricate in order to achieve a desired result. We have to change individual minds and remind people that, even though it may not be the popular thing to do, the right thing to do is support our blue lives—or, at the very least, leave them the hell alone so they can do their jobs. God knows, the people who are the most critical of cops certainly aren't going to wear the badge anytime soon.

So where do we go from here? We live in our communities, interconnected but divided, as we just try to get through each day, hoping we don't have to call the cops for whatever reason. Maybe that hope stems from fear of our neighbors, that they might endanger us or our families, steal our belongings, or harm our children. Or maybe it stems from fear of the cops themselves, and for what they might do when they show up. Maybe we've seen footage of police brutality, or traffic stops gone wrong, or lapses in judgment where an officer just plain fucked up.

For those who are afraid to pick up that phone and call 911 for help, you deserve better. You do. You deserve to feel safe in your home, and safe in your community, and you are worthy of the protection of trusted law enforcement. That is your right as a citizen of this country and, if I have anything to do with it, we will reach that point where Americans feel safe again no matter which side of the law they're on.

Remember, fear sells. Fear produces ratings. Fear acquires votes. We're being manipulated to believe that the police are coming for us, and the only salvation we have from that impending doom is to vote certain people into office who will vanquish our enemy with one stroke of a pen. Give me a break. We're nine months into 2021 and, so far, the promises made by the new administration have gone unfulfilled. And it's not looking good for the remaining three years and three months.

The "cops against society" movement isn't a lone battle; it's just one of hundreds being fought in the US every day. The numbers are staggering but, because of the way the media works, you typically won't see them until a tragedy occurs (which is increasing annually, in case that's not glaringly obvious). Just in 2020 alone, the Southern Poverty Law Center (SPLC) tracked 838 individual hate groups in America. They have a section on their site called "Hate Map" where you can click on different states and see a breakdown of each group's imprint. How many does your state have? Do you know about them?

QAnon, Proud Boys, Nation of Islam, neo-Nazis, ACT for America, New Black Panther Party, VDARE, Patriot Front, Antifa, Trumpists, Black Lives Matter, White Lives Matter. Maybe you've heard of these and maybe you haven't. Maybe you support some of them and maybe you don't. But they're out there, hard at work to spew their filth. These groups seek to separate us further, to break us down into ineffectual fragments incapable of creating any meaningful change. They pull us apart at the seams.

What each of these groups forgets is that we're all just people. We have loved ones, bills to pay, and favorite cereals. We have bad days and sore backs. We get out of bed each morning and wonder what kind of day it's going to be. We raise our kids and change our oil and complain about the weather. Some of us go to work and put on a nametag, or an apron, or yes, even a badge. We're all just trying to make it through until bedtime so we can start over tomorrow and, God willing, enjoy some time with our friends and family to experience a little happiness before we die.

I'm not trying to bullshit you into thinking we should all just join hands and live happily ever after; there are massive issues all around us that aren't going away anytime soon. But we can try. We can calm down. We can do better. We can stop crucifying anyone with an opinion a little different from our own. We can stop being dicks in the grocery store, or the gas station, or the parking lot. We can help each other out. We can show a little compassion or tolerance, at the very least.

I can't change the world all on my own, but I can do this: if you're a police officer who feels silenced, reach out to me. If you're a cop who feels marginalized, you are not alone. If you're someone who, like me, got sent down the shit-chute by administrators who said they had your back until it mattered, and you're sitting there staring at that blank wall with a counseling pamphlet on the nightstand, call me. Because I've been through all that, and I somehow made it out, but there are many—too many—who don't. I can't promise I can fix anything, but I can listen. I can give you someone to tell your story to, and maybe we can work together to make some progress in the uphill climb against the trend of cop-hating and the targeting of hard-working men and women in law enforcement.

I can stand with you and, as it turns out, so can all the people who stand with me. Thanks to that TikTok video and some publicity, I now have over 580,000 followers across all my social media accounts, and the numbers grow by the hour. It's no 50 million, but maybe someday. My GoFundMe account—the one my friend started to help recover my lost wages—just passed $540,000. It's still up and running as we speak, because why not? Don't get me wrong, I'm going to use some of it. If you have a problem with that, I'll refer you to the hundreds of donation comments stating, "This money is yours, Nate! Don't give it away!" Talk to them about it. It sounds like a lot of money, and it is, but it's more about what the money represents: people are angry. They're angry about how cops are treated, how unfairly the deck is stacked against them, and how rabidly the media demonizes them and wants to keep them silenced.

From my perspective, the majority of citizens care about and want police officers in their communities.

If you're angry about police, regardless of your reason, talk to me about it. By the time this book lands, I should have my website up and running:

www.officernate.com

The site will be a hub for various things, such as the book order link (tell your friends), some merchandising stuff I'm working on, links to my previous interviews, my social media platforms, my upcoming series of YouTube podcasts and speaking engagements, and even some tutorials on building confidence and learning self-defense (particularly women's self-defense techniques). I plan to highlight an "Officer of the Week" in my ongoing mission to humanize the badge. And yes, I'm still going to do TikToks. All my social media is geared toward the end of advocating for police officers who don't have voices.

There will also be a link to a separate site for the Blue Funds Foundation (you're damn right that acronym is BFF). This will be the nonprofit organization I'd like to direct everyone's generosity toward. The way it will work is that we'll accept applications from marginalized or displaced cops who got the shaft because their departments failed to back them or threw them under the bus for doing their jobs. Cases will be carefully evaluated, eventually by a board or panel of like-minded volunteers, to determine whether said officer is eligible to receive benefits from the foundation, whether that be covering a couple weeks of suspended pay, legal fees, or even medical bills such as counseling needs. We obviously don't want to give money to bad cops who've broken the law, thus the application process. We want to help out the good ones. Bad cops can fuck off.

If you want to support cops like me, funnel those donations into Blue Funds. The more you give, the more we can do.

And, because police officers have such a strong tendency to bury their emotions, hide their pain, and never ask for help, entries can be nominated by loved ones or even concerned citizens. If you're a LEO spouse and see your significant other in dire straits, send me an application and I promise to do my best to lessen that burden. If you have a buddy who got the short end of the stick from a supervisor, let's see if he qualifies for some assistance. And hell, if you're a bad cop and want to know how to change, maybe I can help with that too.

If you're someone who believes officers should do better, maybe you'll agree that we should take better care of them. It's my experience that people do better when they are incentivized rather than penalized. Are you going to leave the brick on the accelerator of the fancy car without changing the oil or tires? How long do you expect officers to keep their head down while they're being whipped with your harsh criticism?

Don't misunderstand me: I think the majority of our officers are doing a damn fine job of protecting and serving. Some people, on the other hand, despite all the training, the hard work, the sacrifice, stress, and trauma our officers endure, are still going to judge them from an armchair. No matter how much crime officers prevent, how many criminals they apprehend, or how many lives they save, they'll never be able to live up to impossible standards. So what's the point of demanding more from them? Will it ever be good enough? If what they do isn't good enough for you now, chances are, it never will be. Perhaps you should put on the uniform and try to do what they do.

One particular failure in the law enforcement profession is on the part of the various agencies to have done next to nothing to help protect the mental health of our officers. Think about what is required and expected of cops, then consider the things they witness throughout their careers, like traffic crash fatalities, child neglect and abuse, child homicides, child suicides, child sexual exploitation, rape cases, sex trafficking. Those things take a toll on the officers who investigate them. Day after day, an officer absorbs all of the evil and darkness one can possibly think to pack into a twelve-hour shift. Then they get spit on, called racist, called corrupt. People wish death upon them and their families, simply for wearing the badge. After all of this, wouldn't it make sense to provide them with some professional help to purge themselves of all the sinister things they see happening in the world? Apparently not, because those resources are not readily available to officers. But there has never been a greater need for them.

March 17th, 2009, I had just checked into service for night watch. A good friend of mine, who was a narcotics detective at the time, asked me if I wanted to help him serve a felony warrant. Of course I did. So we geared up and headed to the Dunes Motel in Twin Falls, Idaho.

The Dunes Motel was a locus of drug activity, and consequently, a familiar sight for most local cops. We had arrested a lot of people out of that motel over the years, so it was no surprise that our warrant was holed up there.

The detective had an informant watching the room; in fact, he was the one who had called in to report that our suspect was in Room #2. When we arrived, the informant confirmed that no one had left the room after the suspect had entered. We showed the informant a photo of the wanted man to confirm it was indeed the person he saw enter the room. It was. We knocked on the door. No answer. We obtained a key from the manager and entered the room.

There were two people in the bedroom. The man we were looking for had hidden himself in the bathroom. With my firearm drawn, I gave him commands to exit the bathroom and advised him of his warrant. After several commands, he rushed out of the bathroom.

The detective and sergeant that had entered the room with me were dealing with the other two occupants as our wanted person tried to bolt past me and out the front door. I grabbed the front of his hoodie and attempted to pull him to the ground, which was difficult while holding a gun in my other hand. He resisted and still tried pushing past me to get out the front door. I pinned him up against the wall next to the exit. That's when he brought his pistol up and pointed it at my face.

That was the moment I realized he had a gun; he'd hidden it behind his leg as he'd run out of the bathroom. I moved my head off-line, grabbed his gun hand, and fired a round into his chest.

He didn't react like they do in the movies. He didn't fly into the wall. Blood didn't splatter on the wall behind him. After reading the autopsy report a few weeks later, I learned that the round I had fired into his chest had severed his right ventricle, and he had been bleeding to death internally. However, he also had meth running through his system, and he continued to fight despite the wound.

He shoved me back and I tripped over some clutter in the middle of the room. While I was on the ground, the detective tackled the suspect as he attempted to flee. I heard four gunshots.

Fuck, he just shot the detective! my mind screamed as I got back to my feet. The suspect got up and ran through the parking lot. I stood in the doorway and fired several more rounds at his back. He went down in the parking lot and died on the spot.

I later learned that the four gunshots I'd heard came from another patrol officer who had arrived just as I fired my first round inside the room. When the officer saw the suspect exiting the room with his gun, the officer commanded him to get on the ground. When he didn't comply, the officer fired, perceiving him as a deadly threat and believing he was the one who had fired the gunshot inside the motel room. The entire incident, from the time we entered the room until the last shot was fired, lasted thirteen seconds.

When "shots fired" goes out over the radio, officers from every surrounding agency haul ass to the scene. If you have been or are currently in law enforcement, you know the feeling that overtakes you when that phrase comes through your earpiece. The call means lives are at stake right at that moment. You could be sitting at the station typing a report, eating a sandwich in your patrol car, or on a call for service. When you hear "shots fired" and you sense the urgency in the voice of the officer who transmitted it, you literally drop everything you're doing and go. You can't get to your patrol car fast enough, you can't get out of the parking lot fast enough, and everything feels like an obstacle preventing you from reaching the scene.

If you're one of the officers already on scene when shit gets real, the sea of red and blue lights approaching, along with the sound of wailing sirens, is the greatest feeling in the world. Your brothers and sisters are coming to help you.

During this incident, city, county, and state officers showed up within minutes. There were four of us present during the shooting. We were all instructed not to talk to each other about the incident. Another detective came to me and said, "Call your attorney"—not because I did anything wrong, but because this was now a homicide investigation and it's only wise to have legal counsel as you go through the process. We were sequestered in a local hotel (not the Dunes). My attorney arrived shortly after and I explained the entire incident to him. The state police were assigned to investigate the shooting. They came to my room and took photographs of me. They took my gun and my magazines. At that time, we were equipped with audio recorders, which they also took.

They didn't interview us until a few days later; traumatic events are easier to recall accurately after some time has passed. We weren't permitted to talk about the incident until after our interviews with the investigators were complete. Now, it might seem silly to some, but we were all eager to talk to each other; each of us had had a different vantage point of the incident. For instance, the detective in the room with me had no idea I scuffled with the suspect. He had no idea I shot the suspect in the chest. He didn't even hear the shot. Our brains do tricky things during high-pressure, life-threatening incidents, because they're too busy trying to survive.

They contracted with a shrink to come in and speak to us as a group—not individually. I don't know if they couldn't afford his rate for the time it would have taken to talk to each of us privately, or if he was just too busy and needed to get to his next appointment. But I don't know anyone who is comfortable enough to express their true feelings about taking a life in a group setting, even when members of that group were involved in the same incident. The session lasted about thirty minutes, and the only good part about it was we all finally got the chance to hear everyone else's perspective from the incident. I tell that story to preface just how little value our department placed on our mental wellbeing. We needed more than the steps they took.

Of course, we were cleared in that shooting. No criminal charges were filed against any of the officers involved, and it was deemed a justifiable homicide. But it's not an event I talk about in any boastful way. The only reason it's here is to prove my point. Taking a life is not something I look on with any sort of pride or sense of nobility; my fellow officers and I did what we needed to do that night to get home to our families, plain and simple. This incident was just one of countless others that contributed to my own mental health struggles. If I'd had the resources and the opportunity to receive treatment throughout my career, perhaps I could have prevented the breakdown I described in an earlier chapter. But that wasn't in the department's budget. The city needed to ensure the city manager had a brand-new office in a brand-new building overlooking Main Avenue. He also needed two deputy city managers to share his workload, whatever the hell that was. We had to send the chief to a "One City" training for the fourth time and spend around $200,000 on a new concept that wasn't even implemented. The premise of "One City" was that some of the decision-making power would filter down into the lower ranks so that those employees would be empowered to determine how city resources were used, and how the individual departments would function, especially where it affected those front-line employees directly.

What a fucking joke.

Can you imagine any captain or chief relinquishing any sort of power or authority? Neither could I, and they didn't, despite spending hundreds of thousands of dollars to send this chief to receive the training for it. I imagine, for that amount of money, the department could have contracted with a very qualified mental health professional who could work with officers in their time of need.

Alas, the individuals who make decisions like that have their own self-interests in mind, while the officers who are working in the blood and the mud are left to foot the bill for their own therapy, assuming there's any money left over at the end of the month. Maybe they can work more overtime in order to cover the extra expense. And people wonder why some officers self-medicate and commit suicide.

Hopefully, by now you've at least caught a glimpse of what officers experience, both on and off the job. If, after reading all this, you still have the urge to shout, "Police reform!" or "Fuck the police!" I'm not sure what else I can do for you. It's not uncommon for people who are wrong to never realize it or acknowledge it. It's also not uncommon for people who need help the most to deny the help being offered. You want me to believe that law enforcement as a whole is corrupt to its core and inherently racist; I can tell you from firsthand experience that is unequivocally false. The more you stomp your feet and label me a racist because I'm not willing to join you in condemning my brothers and sisters in blue, the more foolish you look.

Remember that house I described earlier? The one where the dad OD'd and the kids are huddled together in the back room? Those children, sitting in their own feces, cry and clamor for their neglectful parents because they've been conditioned to believe that's as good as it will get for them. They don't see the filth they're surrounded by, or the impact it has on them. They've been raised to think that their reality is the only one possible. As harmful and nightmarish as it is, they don't realize there's a much safer and healthier world out there where they can thrive.

Those who rant and rail against the police don't know any better; they're just like those poor kids. It's all they've known, and nothing will change unless good people intervene. They need us. They need us to open that door, to carry them out of their toxic mindsets and into the light where they can finally begin to see the men and women of police work for the people they are.

If you're someone who hates cops, I ask you to stop. Stop clamoring for hatred, intolerance, entitlement, and a lack of accountability. We are a nation of laws, and those laws will be enforced. Let go of this white-knuckle grip on a fallible narrative. It's time for each person to accept personal responsibility for his or her own actions, and to stop claiming oppression and victimization as a consequence of race or ethnicity. You are not oppressed; you are lazy and entitled. When a true officer comes to hold you accountable for crimes you've committed, it's not because of the color of your skin; it's because of your actions. Officers don't see color on the streets.

As for the rest of you, thank you for your support. Thank you for standing alongside me to combat the scourge of wokeism that is working to tear our country apart. To the officers, former and current, thank you for your service. Take care of yourselves. Be safe out there. We got your six!

BIBLIOGRAPHY

1. Davis, Hunter. 2020. "Police officer suicide rate more than doubles line-of-duty deaths in 2019, study shows." *Fox News*, January 14, 2020. https://www.foxnews.com/us/texas-police-officer-suicide-rate

2. http://www.lapdonline.org/rampart_most_wanted_content_basic_view/1657

3. Burnham, Bo, dir. *Chris Rock: Tamborine*. Netflix, 2018. https://www.netflix.com/title/80167498.

4. Harrell, Erika and Elizabeth Davis. 2020. "Contacts Between Police and the Public, 2018 – Statistical Tables." Bureau of Justice Statistics, December 2020. https://bjs.ojp.gov/library/publications/contacts-between-police-and-public-2018-statistical-tables.

5. Worldometer. 2021. "Countries in the world by population (2021)." Accessed July 26, 2021. https://www.worldometers.info/world-population/population-by-country/.

6. Social Blade. 2021. "Top 50 Most Followed Twitter Accounts (Sorted By Followers Count)." Accessed July 26, 2021. https://socialblade.com/twitter/top/50/most-followers.

7. The Plain View Project. 2019. "Home." Accessed July 26, 2021. https://www.plainviewproject.org/.

8. Hudson Jr., David L. 2019. "Pickering Connick test." *The First Amendment Encyclopedia*, Accessed July 26, 2021. https://mtsu.edu/first-amendment/article/596/garcetti-v-ceballos).

9. Hudson Jr., David L. 2009. "*Garcetti v. Ceballos* (2006)." *The First Amendment Encyclopedia*, Accessed July 26, 2021. https://mtsu.edu/first-amendment/article/596/garcetti-v-ceballos).

10. (Snyder v. Phelps, 562 U.S. 443, 453 (2011))

11. (Connick v. Myers, 461 U.S. 138, 147–148, 103 S.Ct. 1684, 75 L.Ed.2d 708 (1983))

12. (Munroe v Central Bucks Sch. Dist., 805 F.3d 454, 467 (3d Cir. 2015))

13. The Plain View Project. 2019. "About the Project." Accessed July 26, 2021. https://www.plainviewproject.org/about.

14. Clarke, Rachel and Mariano Castillo. 2014. "Michael Brown shooting: What Darren Wilson told the Ferguson grand jury." CNN, November 26, 2014. https://edition.cnn.com/2014/11/25/justice/ferguson-grand-jury-documents/)

15. Patrick, Robert. 2014. "Darren Wilson's radio call shows fatal encounter was brief." *St. Louis Post-Dispatch*, November 14, 2014. https://www.stltoday.com/news/multimedia/special/ darren-wilson-s-radio-calls-show-fatal-encounter-was-brief/ html_79c17aed-0dbe-514d-ba32-bad908056790.html

16. Shaw, Adam. 2020. "Dozens of federal law enforcement officers in Portland doxed amid riots, officials say." *Fox News*, July 22, 2020. https://www.foxnews.com/politics/dozens-federal-lawenforcement-officers-portland-doxed

17. Valerio, Mike, Laura Wainman, and Nick Boykin. 2021. "MPD confidential officer files obtained in cyber attack, acting Chief Contee says." *WUSA9*, April 29, 2021. https://www.wusa9.com/article/news/local/dc/confidential-police-information-compromised-cyber-attack/65-0bba9ff0-e45d-410f-8af9-a227d778ed7d.

18. Ashford, Brielle. 2021. "Man asks DC police if they'll kill him like Ma'Khia Bryant, officer responds 'are you gonna stab somebody like her?'" *WUSA9*, April 25, 2021. https://www.wusa9.com/article/news/local/makhia-bryant-shooting-mpd-officer-asked-if-he-would-kill-responds-are-you-gonna-stab/65-daffc2b1-25cf-4c38-b23c-260807cbfecf

ABOUT THE AUTHOR

Nate Silvester is a former Idaho police officer who gained national attention—and millions of views—for his controversial TikTok videos. Before his dismissal in 2021, he loyally served the Twin Falls and Bellevue police departments over the course of 13 years. Nate currently lives in Idaho with his daughter and is working hard to establish a non-profit organization to help displaced police officers. Find him online at *www.officernate.com*.

VOYAGE

Voyage Books is the biography and memoir imprint of
Di Angelo Publications.

Di Angelo Publications is a modern publishing firm with
a multicultural team of varied political, secular, and non-
secular beliefs. As an independent publisher, Di Angelo
Publications staunchly supports the First Amendment
and, thus, encourages all of its authors to speak out in
the manner of their choosing. We provide an inclusive
platform for a diverse range of impactful experiences and
unique perspectives. In short, we publish powerful stories.

Founded in 2008, DAP features ten imprints covering
a wide range of topics. Di Angelo Publications' creative
headquarters are in Houston, Texas, while the distribution
warehouse is in Twin Falls, Idaho.

All printing and manufacturing for DAP books is proudly
done in The United States of America.

Learn more about the independent publisher at
www.diangelopublications.com.

DI ANGELO PUBLICATIONS
A Modernized Publishing Firm